MW00876772

Curries and Kababs

Curries and Kababs

✦

Indian Recipes Spiced with Reminiscences

Dipali Sen

iUniverse, Inc.
New York Lincoln Shanghai

Curries and Kababs
Indian Recipes Spiced with Reminiscences

Copyright © 2007 by Dipali Sen

All rights reserved. No part of this book may be used or reproduced by any means, graphic, electronic, or mechanical, including photocopying, recording, taping or by any information storage retrieval system without the written permission of the publisher except in the case of brief quotations embodied in critical articles and reviews.

iUniverse books may be ordered through booksellers or by contacting:

iUniverse
2021 Pine Lake Road, Suite 100
Lincoln, NE 68512
www.iuniverse.com
1-800-Authors (1-800-288-4677)

Because of the dynamic nature of the Internet, any Web addresses or links contained in this book may have changed since publication and may no longer be valid.

The views expressed in this work are solely those of the author and do not necessarily reflect the views of the publisher, and the publisher hereby disclaims any responsibility for them.

Cover art and illustrations by Stacey A. Kaelin
Author photo by Mr. Robert Lagerstrom

ISBN: 978-0-595-46158-5 (pbk)
ISBN: 978-0-595-90458-7 (ebk)

Printed in the United States of America

For my sons Sunasir and Anik, my daughter-in-law Rosemary, my grandchildren Alexander and Annabel.
In memory of my late husband Satu Sen.
This book is also dedicated to all those who have been mentioned in it.

Acknowledgement

I am deeply grateful to my friend Clifford Browder, without whose help this book would have never seen light of day. His tireless guidance, enduring support, and endless enthusiasm helped me to complete it. I also thank my grandchildren Alexander and Annabel, two prolific poets, who kindly gave permission to include two of their poems. Last but not the least, my thanks to Stacey Kaelin, a long-time friend and a gifted artist for the illustrations and cover design.

Contents

RICE

Introduction

Stacey Kaelin

About Indian Cuisine

The phrase "Indian cuisine" casts a spell of aromatic flavor. Its aroma has crossed the boundaries of the Indian subcontinent and spread the world over. Pilafs, curries, kababs, and chutneys are now savored by many people throughout the world, and have a permanent place in many Western kitchens.

India is now the largest democratic country in the world, with a population of over one billion and one of the world's fastest growing economies. There are many regions, each with its own history, culture, and cuisine. I come from Calcutta, which is located in West Bengal on the banks of the river Hooghly, a tributary of the Ganges, on the monsoon-drenched east coast of India. Calcutta is not far from the Sunderbans, an impenetrable jungle on the Bay of Bengal where the Royal Bengal tigers still roam. It was the British capital of India until 1912, and today is the capital of the state of West Bengal. In the late nineteenth and early twentieth centuries, it was also the center of the National Independence Movement to overthrow British rule.

West Bengal—or Bengal, as it was known in undivided India before the partition into India and Pakistan in 1947—is the home of the Bengalis, a food-loving people whose cuisine is very different from that of the rest of the country. Rice is their staple food, and their love for fish is legendary. Fish are abundant in rivers, ponds, and lakes. A Bengali meal is never complete without fish, and of all fish, silvery hilsa is the most prized.

I never went to cooking school. I first learned to cook from my mother and grandmother, who mostly cooked Bengali dishes. I remember my mother, an excellent cook, preparing ordinary family dinners or meals for festive occasions. My grandmother had the magic touch of transforming a simple dish into gourmet fare. I remember her supervising the cooks and organizing meals for her large joint family in the sleepy little town of Bogra, now in East Bengal or Bangladesh, where I spent six years of my childhood. It seems only the other day when, as a small child, I watched her making mouthwatering pithas, pulie, naru, and burfies. These are a specialty of Bengal, found nowhere else; preparing them is complicated and is now a dying art.

India has been invaded many times over the centuries—by Alexander the Great, the Mongols under Genghis Khan, the Mughals, and later by the Portuguese, the French, and the British—and many of these invaders have influenced Indian cuisine. My mother and grandmother taught me Mughlai cuisine—the cuisine of the Mughals, Muslim invaders who first came to India in the sixteenth century. Later I became a pupil of my Goan cook Ben Gomez. From him I learned to make flaky pastry, creampuffs, and pâté à choux, and the art of cutting julienne strips, and above all how to make a soufflé as light as a feather.

Food is connected with people, place, and memory. A symbol of celebration, it brings back to me impressions of people I knew or a sound or a sight from an occasion in my past. When presenting a recipe, often I will include memories and associations—personal, cultural, and historical—that are linked to it in my mind. Readers will hear of dancing girls and monsoon rains and mangoes, a floating palace, the magic of kerosene lamps, a cowherd festival, a celebration of independence, screeching bats, an elephant, and a cobra. While learning to cook Indian cuisine, they will get to know me a little, and the India where I grew up. These are all unforgettable experiences through which I acquired my love, imagination, and enthusiasm for culinary art.

Cooking Indian food can be easy and simple, as I endeavor to demonstrate in this book. All ingredients are available in any Indian grocery, and tedious chores can be avoided by the use of modern kitchen gadgets. I wish success to those who are eager to cook Indian food, and hope they will find this book easy to follow.

Some Tips for Getting Started

Some standard kitchen gadgets are helpful for preparing Indian food: a **food processor, coffee grinder,** and **cheese grater**. Onions, ginger, and garlic can be made into a smooth puree in a food processor; fresh ginger can be grated through a cheese grater with an excellent result.

Ghee, or clarified butter, improves the taste of food. Ghee is a semi-liquid form of butter without water or solid milk contents.

For a cooking medium **canola oil** or **olive oil** can be used. In Bengal, mustard oil is used for most of the cooking, especially to cook fish.

Indian cooking involves many **herbs and spices**. In this book I have used a few basic ones like cumin, coriander, cloves, cinnamon, cardamom, turmeric, and chili. Spice seeds should be ground fresh in a coffee grinder to get the maximum flavor, instead of using readymade powder off the shelves, which tends to lose its full aroma. Toast the seeds in a preheated skillet for a minute or two, stirring constantly and shaking the skillet, until the aroma comes out, while taking care not to burn them. When they have cooled, put them in a grinder and make a powder, which will give full aroma. Turmeric and chili are difficult to grind, so packaged turmeric and chili powders will work. In India spices are combined with a little water and ground to a paste on a grinding stone.

Coconut milk adds a rich and distinctive taste to curries and other dishes. Canned coconut milk can be used to avoid extracting milk from a fresh coconut.

Breads of India

Breads are eaten more in the northern wheat-growing regions of India than in the eastern regions on the Gangetic delta along the Bay of Bengal, where rice grows in abundance and many varieties are cultivated.

India offers more than fifty different types of bread, each with a taste of its own. Breads are one of the main courses in daily meals. They are made of whole wheat flour and water kneaded into a soft dough, rolled out with a rolling pin, and cooked or baked, as the method requires. Most of them are cooked in cast-iron skillets, except for *tandoori naan* and *roti*. Indian breads can be classified mainly into *chappati* or *roti*, plain or stuffed *parathas, tandoori, phulka, kulcha, and luchi.*

Chappati or roti is flat, unleavened bread. The dough is made of finely milled whole wheat flour and water kneaded into a soft dough, rolled very thin, and cooked in a dry skillet. This is the common daily bread, providing the natural goodness of whole wheat; it is excellent for weight watchers.

Paratha, a richer, multi-layered version, is an exquisite flat bread cooked in ghee or oil. *Paratha,* which came to India with Mughal cuisine, can be plain or stuffed. Vegetables like potatoes, green peas, spinach, cauliflower, or onion are cooked with spices and stuffed inside a *paratha* to make a delightful gourmet food. Ground meat or eggs can be used for stuffing as well; there are endless varieties.

Tandoori breads such as naan and roti are baked in a tandoor oven, a cylindrical clay oven used with a charcoal fire. They are soft and retain all their juices and are therefore considered healthy and nutritious.

Phulka and **kulchas** are deep-fried, fluffy breads.

Luchi is Bengal's favorite. Made of flour, it is deep fried in ghee or oil and becomes fluffy like a balloon. It is a delicacy.

There are also a number of lesser known breads like pistachio-flecked gauzban, and a host of other types.

Indian breads should be eaten with the fingers. In India eating is considered sensual, and one should be able to enjoy it through all the senses of taste, smell, sight, and touch. The touch of sensitive fingers stimulates the taste buds, which in turn enhance the taste of food. Only the right hand is used in eating, never the left. Eating with the hand is considered hygienic, as hands are always washed thoroughly before and after a meal, and are probably cleaner than any cutlery. On a visit to India the Shah of Iran, Mohammad Reza Pahlavi, once said, "To eat with a knife and a fork is like making love through an interpreter."

Rice

Rice, the Staple Food of India

Traveling by rail between Calcutta and Bogra, where my grandparents lived, through the train window I saw vast rice fields being tilled by farmers. The farmers wore large straw hats and worked in the fields with plough and cattle under a very hot sun. Some were busy cutting crops with sickles and putting them in piles to be taken to the villages for threshing; later the grain would be husked by women. Sometimes, in the far distance, I saw their mud huts with thatched roofs in the midst of coconut, palm, and banana trees, and small children who watched the passing trains and waved at us; often I waved back. I never tired of these sights.

In India rice is normally sown before monsoon, the rainy season, and harvesting begins after monsoon in autumn, when paddy fields are filled with golden crops. Monsoon starts in mid-May and continues till September or even October. In Bengal it comes during the months of Ashar and Sraban. Late in the afternoon the sky is overcast, thunder roars, and down comes rain, flooding everything. Crops are often damaged by heavy rain, but if the rainfall is less than normal, they are damaged by the blazing sun and lack of water. Dams and irrigation systems have minimized the calamity, but crops in India still largely depend on rainfall.

In Indian villages harvesting is a season of work and happiness. The farmers are busy tilling the fields with the help of cattle, but soon it is time for the harvest festival, when they celebrate the coming of autumn and the abundance of grains. In modern India methods of harvesting have been changed through modern technologies. Tractors, pumps, mechanized irrigation systems, and discharge of accumulated rainwater have brought higher agricultural yields. Even with all this modernization, and the transition to high-yield mechanical farming, many Indian farmers are still practicing traditional farming with plough and cattle. There are many things in India that never change.

Rice is grown extensively in India, but West Bengal, Uttar and Madhya Pradesh, Bihar, and Orissa are the main rice-producing states. Rice is the staple food for more than two-thirds of the population. Bengalis eat rice every day, and poor people and laborers, farmers, and shepherds start the morning with a meal of *pantha bhat*, boiled rice soaked overnight in water, which they eat with salt and chili. There are numerous varieties of rice cultivated in India, but Basmati (meaning "Queen of Fragrance"), with its nutlike flavor and aroma, and long, slender grains, is the world's most sought-after rice; it is cultivated in the foothills of the Himalayas. In India rice is generally classified by the size of the grain. <u>Long grain</u>, long and slender, stays separate and fluffy after cooking; <u>medium grain</u>, shorter and plumper, and <u>short grain</u>, almost round, stick together when cooked.

And what was I doing in Bogra during monsoon, while this life-sustaining crop was growing under heavy rain in the fields? Safe and dry inside, through the window I watched clouds gathering in the sky, then flashes of lighting accompanied by deep rumbles of thunder, and people running for shelter from the torrential rain, while their umbrellas were blown away by strong, gusty winds. These downpours lasted for quite a while, but when they stopped, the sky cleared, and occasionally a rainbow appeared. After the rain I liked to hear frogs singing, and then, at night, watched the moon dancing in and out of the clouds.

My Great-Grandfather Lived like a Sultan

My great-grandfather had a stately mansion in Dacca (now capital of Bangladesh), with a large number of servants consisting of *khansamas* or cooks, *abdars* or servants, and *shahsis,* or coachmen. He used to adorn himself with gems and bathed in rose water. He also imported a nightingale from Persia to sing to him every night before he went to sleep. My father told us many stories about him, especially how he celebrated all the Hindu festivals on a grandiose scale.

Summer was the time for kite flying, and this event always ended on the day when Vishkarma, the god of tools, was worshipped. On that day the sky was filled with kites of many colors, but the main attraction was kite fights. It takes two to fly a kite: one holds the wooden spool with strings, and the other flies the kite either from the roof of a house or from an open field. A special kind of string coated with *manja,* a finely powdered glass mixed with glue and color, is used for kite fights. In the fights each participant tries to cut the string of his opponent's kite. The sharper the *manja,* the better the chance to cut an opponent's string.

Many of my great-grandfather's relatives, friends, and followers participated in the kite fights from the roof of his house. The fights ended at sunset, and all the kite fighters were entertained with a lavish dinner. Several dishes of fish, meat, vegetables, and sweets were prepared. Pilaf cooked with meat or chicken is called Biriyani. My great-grandfather loved all kinds of Biriyani pulao, and this he used to order very often.

Lamb Biriyani

Serves 4-5
2-inch cinnamon stick, broken into small pieces
6 cloves
½ teaspoon cardamom seeds, crushed
1 tablespoon poppy seeds
2 onions, chopped

2 tablespoons grated ginger
4 cloves garlic, minced
2 lbs. lamb, medium-size pieces
1 cup plain yogurt
2 cups basmati rice
¼ cup ghee
Salt to taste
4 medium onions, sliced
½ teaspoon saffron, soaked in 1 tablespoon milk
½ teaspoon grated nutmeg
4 hardboiled eggs, each one quartered lengthwise
1/2 cup golden raisins, lightly sautéed
¼ cup pistachios, halved
¼ cup almonds, blanched and halved

Put cinnamon, cloves, and cardamom seeds in grinder to make a smooth powder.
Make a separate powder of poppy seeds.
Put 2 chopped onions, ginger, and garlic in blender and make a purée.
Marinate lamb pieces with all the ground spices and the onion, ginger, and garlic purée and the yogurt for a few hours.
Cook rice with 6 cups of water and when ¾ done, drain out excess water. Cook it like spaghetti.
Heat 2 tablespoons ghee in a pot, add marinated lamb, and cook over low heat for 30 minutes or until lamb is tender. Add salt to taste.
Sauté 4 sliced onions in ghee until golden brown and crisp. Remove.
In an oven-proof bowl make a layer of rice at the bottom, and on top of it a layer of lamb (without any gravy) and sautéed onions. Sprinkle with a little soaked saffron.
Make alternate layers of rice and lamb with sautéed onions. Finally add lamb gravy and saffron with additional ghee on top.
Cover very tightly so that steam does not escape. Cook in an oven at 250 degrees for another 30 minutes.
Put in a large serving dish and garnish with hard-boiled eggs, lightly sautéed raisins, pistachios, and almonds.

There was no oven in my great-grandfather's time. An oven was improvised by putting a stainless steel or aluminum or copper pan over a coal fire, and adding additional live coals on top of the lid. The lid was carefully sealed with flour dough.

An Obsession with Green

One of my friends in Calcutta was very fond of the color green. She used green in her home décor and her clothing, and even tried to cook food in green, hence this recipe. I remember her wearing a beautiful emerald necklace on many occasions; it became a symbol of her. This is not only a colorful dish, but also very tasty. A dish for St. Patrick's Day? Just a thought.

Spinach Rice or Green Rice

Serves 4
2 cups basmati rice.
1 lb. fresh spinach or 1 package frozen spinach
1/3 cup oil
1 onion, finely chopped
1 teaspoon grated ginger
1 clove garlic
2 bay leaves
4 cloves
2-inch cinnamon stick, broken into small pieces
4 cardamoms, crushed
Salt to taste

Rinse rice and drain on a paper towel.
Cook spinach in 2 cups of hot water for a few minutes. Put in a blender and mix thoroughly. Add another cup of water. Strain and set aside. Save spinach water.
In a pot heat oil and sauté onion, ginger, and garlic.
Add bay leaves, cloves, cinnamon, and cardamoms and stir for a few seconds.
Add rice and keep stirring over a low flame until rice turns slightly brown.

Add spinach water and let it stand 3 fingers above the rice level.

Add salt. Cover and cook over a very low flame until rice is done and water is completely absorbed. Remove lid and stir rice with a fork to fluff it up. If necessary, put rice in an oven preheated to 350 degrees for a few minutes to dry it and separate the grains.

Consider serving with green napkins!

Untouchables: A Product of the Pernicious Hindu Caste System

According to the ancient sacred literature, the Aryan priests divided the Hindu society into a caste system. They divided the society into four divisions according to the occupations of the people, and placed their own priestly class at the top. This complex social hierarchy consists of four castes: Brahmins, the priestly class; Kshatriyas, warriors and rulers; Vaisyas, farmers and merchants; and Sudras, unskilled laborers and workers. Below these classes are the Untouchables, considered to be outside caste and society, and condemned to live a life of degradation, discrimination, and social segregation. Branded as unclean, they use separate water taps or wells and live in a separate section of a village; even their shadow is considered polluted. They are deprived of occupation opportunities and education, and are forbidden to enter a temple or even to sit in front of a higher caste. Their only occupation is to work as scavengers and clean toilets. If an Untouchable enters a house of a higher caste, any place where he stood must be washed. Hindus believe that to be born as an Untouchable is punishment for sins committed in a previous life, according to their Karma.

Gandhi fought against this social injustice and called them Harijans (children of God). The Indian constitution has granted equal rights to all citizens, and efforts have been taken to eliminate this social and economic injustice by granting equal opportunities and rights, and forbidding discrimination and exploitation on the basis of race, caste, gender, and religion. The Untouchables have been reclassified as "Scheduled Caste" and have been granted special privileges. In 1997 K.R.Narayana, an Untouchable, became the tenth president of India, holding the highest office in the country. Despite all this, even today the prejudice persists, and untouchability still exists in rural India.

My Friend Phuleswari and the Screeching Bats

Phuleswari, which means goddess of flowers, was my friend and constant companion in Bogra. She was my age, and the daughter of my grandfather's coachman. She was an untouchable, but my grandparents never believed in the caste system that prevailed at that time in India, so Phuleswari had unlimited access to our house, and she and I even ate together.

We used to play with dolls, but sometimes we went out looking for adventure. There was a small stretch of road near the river with tall banyan trees on both sides, making the road look like a dark tunnel. Hundreds of bats hung upside down from those trees. Hand in hand we used to go there very quietly to look at them. Sometimes a loud noise startled them, and they made tremendous screeching noises that frightened us and made us run away. But later we recovered our courage and ventured back to look again at the hanging bats.

We were often taken out sailing and watched the river and sky meeting in the far distance, while the fishing boats cast a romantic silhouette against the backdrop of the vast span of water. After my grandfather passed away, I returned to my parents and never saw Phuleswari again. Even today I often think back to my happy childhood days with her in Bogra.

My grandmother often used to make this particular rice dish for us for lunch. It was a comfort food, and when she prepared this dish, the aroma drifted out from the kitchen, making me even hungrier.

Rice with Potatoes

Serves 4
1 cup Basmati rice
1-inch cinnamon stick, broken into small pieces
4 cloves

½ teaspoon cardamom seeds
1 teaspoon cumin seeds
3 tablespoons ghee
2 tablespoons oil
2 potatoes, each cut into 4 pieces
1 teaspoon turmeric powder
½ chili powder
1 tablespoon finely grated ginger
3 bay leaves
1 teaspoon fennel
Salt to taste

Rinse rice and spread on a paper towel to dry thoroughly.
Put cinnamon, cloves, and cardamom seeds in a coffee grinder and make a smooth powder.
Make a smooth powder with cumin seeds separately.

Put oil and 1 tablespoon ghee in a pan and sauté rice and potatoes for two minutes or until rice and potatoes are red. Stir with a spoon to prevent rice from burning. Remove rice from oil and set aside.
Heat 1 tablespoon ghee, add turmeric, chili, cumin powder, and grated ginger with a little water and stir briskly.
Add about 1 ½ cups boiling water, then add rice and potatoes and let boil for 30 seconds.
Lower heat, cover pot, and simmer until rice and potatoes are cooked, and water is completely absorbed.
In another pan heat the remaining 1 tablespoon ghee, add bay leaves and fennel, and stir for a few seconds. Cook over a medium heat for two minutes.
Add cinnamon, clove, and cardamom powder to rice, again mix thoroughly with fork to make it fluffy.
Remove from heat and serve hot.

Pilaf, a Gift from the Mughals

The seasoned rice dish known as pilaf, also called pulao in Bengal, is a perennial favorite. Pilaf came to India with the Mughals in the sixteenth century. Since that time Mughlai food—the food of these Muslim invaders—has become interwoven into the texture of Indian society. No festive occasion is complete without the serving of a pilaf.

Pilaf is cooked with long-grained Basmati rice or a similar aromatic rice. It is sautéed and seasoned before liquid and other ingredients are added. All kinds of delicacies like nuts, spices, meat and poultry, egg, shell fish, or vegetables are added. Often rose water, saffron, and food coloring are used to give a special favor and appearance, so as to make this dish superb.

Fish Pilaf

Here is one of my grandmother's recipes, a combination of rice and fish, which I have modified for modern kitchens.

Fish

6 thick fish fillets
½ cup plain yogurt
Juice of one lemon
2 teaspoons grated ginger
2 cloves garlic, finely chopped
¼ teaspoon each of cinnamon, cloves, and cardamom powder
2 tablespoons oil
Salt to taste
Marinate the fish fillets in all the above ingredients for at least one hour.
Broil in a preheated broiler at 350 degrees for 15 minutes.

Rice

1½ teaspoons cumin seeds
1 tablespoon coriander seeds
1 tablespoon poppy seeds
2 cups Basmati rice
2 tablespoons ghee
Salt to taste
3 bay leaves
1 tablespoon butter
Toast cumin, coriander, and poppy seeds in a dry skillet over a medium flame, stirring briskly, until a rich aroma comes out. Put them in coffee grinder and make a smooth powder.
Put the powder in cheesecloth, make a small pouch, and tie with a string.
In a pot boil 4 cups water. When it comes to boiling point, put pouch in water, and boil until water is reduced by half. Remove pouch and set aside water.
Rinse rice and dry on a paper towel.
Heat 2 tablespoons ghee, and cook rice for 4 to 5 minutes, stirring briskly.
Reduce heat and add spiced water to 3 fingers above rice level.
Add salt to taste, cover tightly, and simmer over low flame until water is completely absorbed, stirring with a fork from time to time.

Coat a deep casserole with butter. Arrange a layer of pilaf, put fish fillets and bay leaves over it, then make a top layer with rest of pilaf. Dot it with butter.

Cover casserole with aluminum foil and place in a preheated oven at 350 degrees for 10 minutes.

Serve this dish with chutney. It is a meal by itself.

Peas Pilaf

Serves 4

This dish brings a feeling of spring and sunshine into the dining room. It is delicious, full of aroma, and a pleasure to look at, yet easy to prepare.

2 cups Basmati rice
4 tablespoons oil
1 ½ teaspoons cumin seeds
2/3 cup fresh shelled green peas or ½ package frozen green peas.
Salt to taste

Rinse rice and dry thoroughly on a paper towel.
In a heavy pot heat oil and add cumin seeds. When cumin seeds start to splutter, add rice and stir constantly until rice turns slightly brown.
Add boiling water 3 fingers above rice level, reduce heat, cover pot, and simmer until rice is almost done.
Add green peas and salt to taste, and cook for another 5 minutes. Mix thoroughly with a fork before serving.

Kitchuree: A Heart-Warming Dish for Rain and Cold Weather

Kitchuree, a combination of rice and lentil, is mainly associated with the monsoon or rainy season in Bengal, which starts in May and ends in September. The monsoon brings heavy rain with thunderstorms and occasional hailstorms. In such weather it is a tradition in Bengal to eat kitchuree with Hilsa fish. Hilsa fish from the River Ganges are extremely delicious but full of fine bones; unless you know how to eat them, you will end up with bones in your throat. When rain is pouring heavily and a howling wind is lashing the windowpanes, kitchuree warms body and soul. Kitchuree is a main dish served at lunch or dinner, or on other occasions as well. There are several kinds of kitchurees cooked in Bengal.

Bhuna Kitchuree

Serves 4
1 cup Moong lentil
1 cup Basmati rice
4 large onions, thinly sliced
1/3 cup oil
1 ½ teaspoons turmeric powder
½ teaspoon chili powder
1 teaspoon cumin seed powder
4 green chilies
1 teaspoon peppercorn
6 cardamoms, bruised
2-inch cinnamon stick, broken into small pieces
Salt to taste

Stir-fry lentil in a dry skillet, stirring constantly for a few minutes. Cool. Rinse lentil and dry on a paper towel.

Rinse rice and dry on a paper towel.

Sauté onions in oil until golden, remove from flame.

In the same oil sauté rice for 2-3 minutes, add lentil, and cook for 7-8 minutes, stirring briskly.

Add onions and sauté for another few minutes.

Add turmeric, chili, cumin powder, peppercorn, cardamoms, cinnamon, and salt. Add just enough hot water to cover rice mixture, then add green chilies, cover pot, and simmer over low heat until rice and lentil are cooked and water is completely absorbed.

Place kitchuree in a preheated oven at 350 degrees for a few minutes before serving. Serve very hot.

A perfect luncheon or supper dish for cold, wintry weather. It was my mother's favorite recipe. What could be better than a plate of steaming kitchuree on a winter night, when you are curled up on a sofa with your favorite book in hand, snow falling silently outside, wind rattling the windowpanes, and a log fire burning brightly nearby. (Incidentally, it does not snow in Bengal. I have drawn a scenario of a snowy night over here.)

A Treat of Pilaf from Iran

When this dish was served at a dinner in my uncle's house in Teheran, I was amazed. My uncle, who headed the Finance Department of the Tata Iron & Steel Company in India, was temporarily stationed in Iran in the mid-1970s during the regime of the Shah. He had an excellent cook and her dishes were fantastic, but this one surpassed them all.

A pilaf in the shape of a cake with a grand visual display, it is an epicurean delight.

Baked Lamb Pilaf

Serves 4
1 large onion, chopped
2 inches fresh ginger, grated
3 cloves garlic
2 cups Basmati rice
2 lbs. boneless lamb, cubed
1 cup plain yogurt
1 ½ teaspoons turmeric powder
2/3 cup oil
6 cardamoms
6 cloves
1 2-inch long cinnamon stick, broken
3 bay leaves
Salt to taste
¼ cup ghee
2 egg yolks
1 teaspoon saffron, dissolved in 2 tablespoons milk

Put chopped onion, grated ginger, and garlic in blender and make into a smooth paste.

Rinse rice and spread on a paper towel to dry.

Marinate lamb cubes in ½ cup yogurt with the onion, ginger, and garlic paste and turmeric powder for 2 hours.

In a pan heat 2 tablespoons oil and add cardamoms, cloves, and cinnamon. Add rice and stir briskly for a few minutes.

Add just enough boiling water to cover rice. Add bay leaves and salt. Bring to a rolling boil, reduce heat, and cover pan.

Simmer over a low flame until rice is cooked and water is completely absorbed.

In another pot heat the rest of the oil, add marinated lamb, and cook until spices separate from oil.

Add a cup of hot water, and salt to taste, and simmer over low heat until lamb is tender and a little gravy remains.

Coat a round casserole with ghee or butter.

Combine ¼ of rice pilaf with egg yolks and 1cup yogurt, mix thoroughly.

Line the casserole bottom and the sides with this rice, egg, and yogurt mixture. This should form into a crust when baked.

Arrange a layer of lamb without gravy, a layer of pilaf on top of that, then another layer of lamb, and finally another layer of pilaf. Add ¼ cup of ghee to it. Combine dissolved saffron and gravy and pour evenly over the pilaf. Cover the casserole.

Bake in a preheated oven at 350 degrees for 30 minutes or until the sides turn brown and form a crust.

Put the round casserole upside down on a round serving dish, and gently tap the top, so that the pilaf comes out on the serving dish. Small round baked potatoes can be arranged around the pilaf cake.

It is a unique and extremely delicious dish.

Meatballs, the Highlight of Roman Feasts

Meatballs, known as *kofta* in India and the Middle East, are said to have graced the tables of the ancient Romans. The earliest mention of meatballs is found in a recipe book written by a cook from the palace of King Herod of the Holy Land during Roman rule. Later in the first century Apicius, the author of a Roman cookbook, gave many recipes that called for ground meat mixed with bread-crumbs and shaped into small balls, resembling our present-day meatballs. This is the only cookbook from that era that survives.

Meatballs are prepared in various ways and are enjoyed by everyone on this planet. In Asian cuisine *koftas* are cooked with spices and herbs. In India *koftas* are also cooked with fish or vegetables, besides ground meat. Here is a recipe for meatballs with pilaf.

Pilaf with Meatballs

Serves 4-5

Meatballs

1-inch cinnamon stick
4 cloves
4 cardamoms
1 lb. ground lamb
¼ cup finely chopped cilantro leaves
½ cup plain yogurt
3 tablespoons oil
1 tablespoon grated ginger
Salt to taste

In coffee grinder make a smooth powder of cinnamon, cloves, and cardamoms.

Put ground meat in a bowl with chopped cilantro, half the powdered spices, 2 tablespoons of yogurt, and salt to taste. Mix thoroughly and make small balls, each about the size of a marble.

Heat oil in a pot, add ginger and rest of spices, and stir over medium heat with a little sprinkling of water. Add remaining yogurt and meatballs.

Simmer over very low heat for fifteen minutes or until gravy completely dries up. Remove from heat and set aside.

Rice

¼ cup oil or ghee
2 cups Basmati rice
4 cloves
2-inch cinnamon stick, broken into small pieces
6 cardamoms, crushed
3 bay leaves
A pinch of salt

Heat oil and cook rice with cloves, cinnamon, and cardamoms for a few minutes.

Add boiling water one inch above rice level. Add bay leaves and a pinch of salt.

Cover pot and simmer for fifteen minutes or until rice is completely cooked and water is absorbed.

Put rice on a serving dish, and garnish with meatballs on top. Serve hot.

Stacey Kaelin

Deepavali or Diwali, a Festival of Lights

One year on the night of *Diwali,* I was invited to a friend's home in Calcutta for dinner and a game of cards. *Diwali* is a festival of lights, and is celebrated in India on the dark new moon night in the Indian month of Kartick (October/November). In Bengal, Kali, the goddess of strength, is worshipped on that night, whereas the rest of India worships Laskhmi, the goddess of wealth. On the night of *Diwali* everyone, poor or rich, decorates their house with rows of *diyas,* earthen lamps or candles, to signify the victory of divine power over evil, and to dispel darkness and bring light and joy into everyone's life. All around my friend's house hundreds of *diyas* were lit, transforming the surroundings into a world of fantasy. Also, thousands of fireworks were set off, lighting up the night sky. Playing cards on the night of *Diwali* is another age-old custom, since gambling then is believed to bring prosperity. My host and all her guests played cards, while firecrackers burst outside.

In addition to lights, fireworks, and gambling, this special evening is the occasion for a feast. After watching fireworks and indulging in a bit of gambling (I didn't win!), we were treated to a sumptuous dinner. The main course was a pilaf dish with several whole roasted spring chickens adorning it. It was a feast to remember.

Pilaf with Roast Spring Chicken

Serves 4
4 very small spring chickens
Salt and pepper to taste
Juice of one lemon
4 tablespoons butter
4 large potatoes, peeled and cut lengthwise into halves
2 cups Basmati rice
1/3 cup oil
1 large onion, thinly sliced

1 tablespoon grated ginger
2 cloves garlic, minced
2 bay leaves
1/3 cup blanched almonds
1/3 cup toasted almonds

Clean chickens thoroughly, and rub with salt and pepper.
Tie legs and wings of chickens with string. Sprinkle lemon juice, dot with butter.
Place chickens in a roasting pan with potatoes and roast in a preheated oven at 350 degrees for 30 minutes or until chickens are tender. Remove, cut off strings, set aside.
Rinse rice and dry on a paper towel.
Heat oil, sauté onion, ginger, and garlic for a minute. Add rice and keep on stirring for a few minutes more.
Add enough boiling water to cover rice, then, add bay leaves and salt to taste.
Cover pot, lower heat, and simmer over a slow heat until rice is cooked and water evaporates.
Add almonds and raisins to rice with a fork. (Forks do not break rice, and they help make rice fluffy.)
Serve rice on a platter and arrange chickens on top with potatoes.

Gravy
Blend 1 tablespoon flour with a little water and add it to the juice from roasting pan. Stir and simmer for a few minutes until gravy thickens.
Serve gravy in a sauceboat.

Stacey Kaelin

My Dancing Peacock

I had a beautiful peacock as a pet in Bogra. It was kept in an enormous pen adjacent to my grandparents' bungalow. The peacock had stunningly beautiful blue-green plumage and a shimmering blue breast. I loved to hear its calls, which were very similar to a cat's *meow*, only much louder. My friend Phuleswari and I watched the peacock all the time, but never dared to go inside the pen. Trying to communicate with it and gain its friendship, we threw fistfuls of grain inside the pen. We watched the peacock coming slowly toward us lifting one foot first, and then the other, looking at us and pondering what to expect from these two little girls. The peacock was fed on grains and a variety of greens.

In one corner of the pen stood a *champa* tree, a species of magnolia, with flowers with waxy white petals. The ground was always strewn with flowers. Most of the time the peacock roamed around the tree looking for worms and insects to feast upon. When the sky was overcast, and rain started to fall, it would open its immense plumage like a fan and dance majestically in rhythmic steps. It could always tell when rain was coming. The memory of that spectacular peacock dancing in rain on the flower-strewn ground is still deeply embedded in my memory.

My grandmother renamed a few dishes after some of my favorite things. I relished a pilaf dish prepared with lots of coconut and golden raisins, so she renamed it "mayur pilaf" (*mayur* = peacock in Bengali). One of my dolls was named after a sweet dish, too. Mayur or peacock pilaf is a very simple dish to cook, and yet so delicious.

Mayur Pilaf

Serves 4-5
2 cups Basmati rice
¼ cup ghee
4 cloves
4 cardamoms, crushed

1-inch piece cinnamon, broken into small pieces
1 can coconut milk
Salt to taste
½ cup shredded coconut
½ cup golden raisins
2 tablespoons almonds

Rinse rice and dry on a paper towel.

Heat ghee, leaving one tablespoon aside, add cloves, cardamoms, and cinnamon, sauté for a few seconds.

Add rice, and continue to stir until rice turns brown, approximately one minute.

Add coconut milk and salt.

Cover pot and simmer on a very low flame until rice is cooked, and coconut milk is absorbed.

In another pan, heat one tablespoon ghee and sauté shredded coconut, raisins, and almonds light brown. Remove and set aside.

Add sautéed coconut, raisins, and almonds to the rice with a fork.

Heat 1tablespoon ghee, add turmeric, chili, cumin powder, and grated ginger with a little water and stir briskly. Add about 1 ½ cup boiling water then add rice and potatoes and let boil for 30 seconds. Lower heat, cover pot, and simmer until rice and potatoes are cooked, and water is completely absorbed.

In another pan heat the remaining 1 tablespoon ghee, add bay leaves and fennel, and stir for a few seconds. Add it to rice and stir with a fork to blend aniseeds. Cook over a medium heat for 2 minutes.

Mix cinnamon, clove, and cardamom powder with rice, again mix thoroughly with a fork to make it fluffy. Remove from flame and serve hot.

Vegetables & Fruits

There Are Lots of Vegetarians in India

One can always tell when winter has arrived in India by the fresh and colorful look of the vegetables and fruits in markets. There one sees firm tomatoes arranged in pyramids, shiny purple eggplants, and green young leaves of spinach of a velvety texture, snow-white cauliflowers, and tender and glistening peas in their pods. The sellers sit beside their wares with their scales. They are friendly and indulge in small talk while selecting and weighing vegetables for customers.

Much of the Indian population is vegetarian. Emperor Ashok popularized vegetarian food in the second century BC. Ashok was the most celebrated and benevolent ruler in ancient India, and his conquests expanded his territory to the four corners of India. But the battle of Kalinga brought a turning point in his life. At the sight of thousands of dead warriors on the battlefield, he became repentant and, renouncing military conquests, embarked on spiritual conquests, turning his attention to the doctrines of Buddha and principles of nonviolence, and to respect for the value of life. Mahavir, the founder of the religion of Jainism, which flourished in India in the sixth century BC, also influenced to a great extent the people's turning to vegetarian food, as did the influence of Buddha.

My Grandmother, a Grande Dame of Cooking

In Bogra we were a large joint family of more than twenty relatives living together in two big houses. The joint family system is an ancient Indian institution where two or three generations live under the same roof and share the same food. This system has been highly valued as the cornerstone of Indian society. Now, with the passing of time, joint families are breaking up and many people live in nuclear families: a couple with their unmarried or dependent children. I lived with my grandparents in a beautiful bungalow surrounded by mango trees, with a huge flower and vegetable garden at the back, while the rest of the family lived in a massive house with a quadrangular courtyard.

My grandmother was the matriarch. She was of medium stature with fine features and very long hair. A person of strong determination and will, and at the same time very affectionate, she was respected and loved by everyone. She was in charge of the kitchen, assisted by other female relatives and a retinue of servants. In the large dining room each of us would sit on a small individual carpet with our back against the wall. At each place small bowls were neatly arranged around plates. Food was served by servants. Children and adults ate together. Mealtime was fun and conversation flowed endlessly.

Our daily lunch and dinner consisted of rice, lentils, vegetables, fish, and chutney, finishing with *misthi dai*, or sweetened yogurt. Here are a few dishes I remember from my childhood.

Eggplant Bharta

Serves 3-4
1 large eggplant
2 tablespoons oil
1 medium onion, chopped
1-inch piece of fresh ginger, grated

2 cloves garlic
1 teaspoon cumin powder
Salt and pepper to taste
A few sprigs of fresh cilantro leaves, finely chopped
1 teaspoon lemon juice

Cut eggplant into halves lengthwise and heat them on stove top. Brown both sides. Let cool, peel off the skin, and with a fork mash eggplant into pulp.
Sauté onion and ginger in 2 tablespoons oil for a few minutes, add garlic, and then add eggplant pulp and cumin powder, and salt and pepper to taste, and stir-fry for a few more minutes.
Remove from flame and add cilantro leaves and lemon juice.

I use this delicious recipe also as a paté and serve it on toasted bread as an hors d'oeuvre.

Fried Okra

Serves 3-4
½ lb. okra, diced, or 1 package frozen okra
3 tablespoons oil
1 teaspoon cumin seeds
1 large onion, finely chopped
1 teaspoon turmeric powder
Salt to taste
¼ teaspoon each of cinnamon, cardamom, and cloves powder

Wash okra if fresh, and dry on a paper towel. Dice into small pieces.
Heat oil, add cumin seeds and then chopped onion, and sauté for one minute.
Add okra and continue sautéing with turmeric powder and salt until okra turns brown and crisp.
Add cinnamon, cardamom, and cloves powder. Remove from flame.

Alur Dum (Potato Curry)

Serves 4-5
1 onion, chopped
1 tablespoon grated ginger
1 lb. potatoes
2 tablespoons oil
1 teaspoon turmeric powder
½ teaspoon chili powder
¼ teaspoon each of cinnamon, cloves, and cardamom, ground
1 teaspoon cumin seeds, ground
2 tablespoons tomato ketchup
2 bay leaves
Salt to taste
½ can coconut milk
1 tablespoon ghee

Blend onion and ginger in a blender and make a purée.
Parboil potatoes and peel. Cut each potato into four pieces.
Heat oil, add onion and ginger puree, then stir, making sure it doesn't get burnt.
Add turmeric, chili, cinnamon, cloves, cardamom, cumin, tomato ketchup, bay leaves, and about 2 tablespoons water. Stir well.
Add potatoes and salt, and continue to cook over a medium heat.
Add coconut milk and ghee, lower heat, and cook until potatoes are done.

This is a dish for potato lovers.

Monsoon Brings a Harvest of Mangoes

In Bogra, where I spent my childhood, there were several mango trees surrounding our two houses. In summer, late in the afternoon suddenly the sky would be overcast with dark clouds, and a storm would blow from all directions, for it was monsoon time in Bengal. Mangoes would start dropping from the trees, covering the ground, and all the children would come running to collect them. It was a thrilling experience.

In summer my grandmother was always busy preparing mango pickles and chutneys and storing them in enormous earthenware vats for year-round consumption. Bottles of chutneys and pickles were sent to friends and neighbors all around town.

Green Mango Chutney

Serves 4
2 tablespoons oil
1 teaspoon cumin seeds
2 green mangoes, peeled and quartered lengthwise
1/3 cup of sugar or more, according to taste
Salt to taste

In a pan heat oil and add cumin seeds. Add mango slices and stir.
Add 2 cups of water, sugar, and salt.
Simmer on a low flame for 15 to 20 minutes or until mangoes become soft and pulpy. Remove and chill thoroughly.

Green Mango Chutney, Another Variation

2 green mangoes, peeled and quartered lengthwise
½ cup vinegar
A pinch of salt
½ cup sugar
¼ cup raisins
2 tablespoons oil
1 teaspoon cumin seeds, ground
1 2-inch cinnamon stick, broken into small pieces
1-inch piece of fresh ginger root, peeled and thinly sliced
Salt to taste

In a bowl mix mango pieces with vinegar, salt, sugar, and raisins, and set aside.
In a pan heat oil and add cumin, cinnamon stick, and ginger, and stir briskly all the time.
Add mango mixture, and another pinch of salt, cover lid, and simmer over a low heat for about half an hour.
Serve cold.

Ripe Mango Chutney

Serves 4

1 can mango pulp
2-inch piece fresh ginger, peeled and chopped
¼ teaspoon salt
¼ cup water
¼ cup sugar or less, according to taste
2 tablespoons oil
1 teaspoon *panch phoran*[1]
2 pieces dry red chilies

In a pan thoroughly mix mango pulp, chopped ginger, salt, and water. Simmer on a low flame, covered, for about 20 minutes.
Add sugar, stir well, and remove from flame.
In a pan heat oil and add *panch phoran*, chopped ginger, red chilies, and mango mixture. Stir for a few minutes and remove from flame.
Serve cold.

These chutneys go well with all kinds of roasts and even with hamburgers!

Mango Fool

This is a summer dish, appropriate for a first course. It is cool and delightfully refreshing. It was one of my Goan cook Ben Gomez's favorite recipes to serve at lunch in summer. He didn't know why it was called "mango fool."

Serves 2
2 large mangoes, cut into cubes without the center stone
½ cup sugar
¼ teaspoon salt
¾ cup heavy cream

Boil mangoes in two cups of water with sugar and salt until mangoes get pulpy and soft.

---

1.   *Panch phoran* is a combination of equal parts of cumin, brown mustard, black cumin, and fenugreek seeds; ask your nearest Indian grocery for it.

Strain through a sieve. Chill thoroughly.

Add cream before serving.

Serve this refreshing dessert in individual cups or bowls.

Stacey Kaelin

Getting Help from the Goddess of Learning

Kool, as plums are called in India, is a popular fruit in Bengal. The season for eating *kool* starts on the day the goddess Saraswati is worshipped, the fifth day of waxing moon in January or February of each year. Saraswati personifies learning, knowledge, wisdom, art, and science, and she is worshipped in Bengali homes, schools, and colleges. Students place books, pens, pencils, and musical instruments in front of the statue of the deity to get her blessings and excel in examinations. In my schooldays mathematics was not my favorite subject, so I made sure that all my math books were placed in front of her. Unfortunately, my math scores did not improve. Saraswatai Puja (*puja* = worship) indicates the start of spring. On that day girls wear orange-colored clothes. It is also an auspicious day for inaugurating a child's first learning. With the help of a parent, a child is encouraged to write a few letters of the alphabet on a slate.

Chutney originated in India. It is a sweet and spicy condiment to enhance the flavor of other dishes.

Plum or Kool Chutney

Serves 4-5

3 tablespoons mustard oil or any other cooking oil
1 teaspoon fennel seeds
3 dry red chilies
1 lb. plums
1 cup sugar
A pinch of salt
½ cup raisins
2 tablespoons finely sliced ginger

Heat oil over a medium heat and add fennel and chilies, then stir and add plums and 1 cup hot water.
Add sugar, cook until mixture gets syrupy.
Add a pinch of salt and raisins. Cook for another 2 minutes.
Add ginger slices and remove.
Cool before serving.

The Splendor of a Floating Palace

Cauliflower roast is not only a gastronomic delight, but also a pleasure to the eye. I first saw it among several other dishes at a luncheon buffet at the Lake Palace Hotel in Udaipur. The Lake Palace Hotel, a unique and opulent hotel, was built by the maharana Jagat Singh II as his summer resort in the 18th century. The white marble palace floats like a swan in the middle of Lake Pinchola, casting its reflection on the shimmering water, with an enchanting surrounding of rolling hills. The summer palace with its Bohemian crystal chandeliers, marble pillars, and carved wooden furniture was later converted into a hotel. A visit to this floating palace takes the guests back to the forgotten days of the ranas of Ragasthan, of which Udaipur is one of the districts. We had a wonderful time in this majestic hotel, and my sons Sunasir and Anik spent most of the time sailing boats on the calm water of the lake.

Cauliflower Roast

Serves 6
1 head of white cauliflower
6 small round potatoes
1 medium onion, chopped
1 tablespoon grated ginger
2 cloves garlic, minced
1 cinnamon stick
4 cloves
½ teaspoon cardamom seeds, crushed
½ cup oil
1 teaspoon turmeric powder
½ teaspoon paprika
Salt to taste

½ cup plain yogurt

In a pot boil cauliflower and potatoes in salted water until half done. Drain and set vegetables aside. Save vegetable water.

Put onion, ginger, and garlic in blender and make a purée.

Grind cinnamon, cloves, and cardamom in a grinder.

In a pot sauté onion, ginger, and garlic purée in oil and stir briskly.

Add turmeric and paprika and continue to stir for a minute.

Add a few spoons of vegetable water. Add salt.

Add cinnamon, cloves, and cardamom powder, and stir over a medium flame until spices separate from oil.

Beat yogurt with a fork, add to spices, and blend thoroughly. Remove spices from flame.

In a shallow pan arrange cauliflower in the center and potatoes all around it, then pour spice mixture over the vegetables.

Bake for 15 to 20 minutes in a preheated oven at 350 degrees.

Calcutta and Its Early Days

Calcutta's early history is connected with the British East India Company, whose merchants first arrived there in the late 17th century. One day one of them, Job Charnock, went to witness the burning of a Hindu widow on her dead husband's funeral pyre. Captivated by the beauty of the Brahmin girl, he rescued her from being burnt and married her—a real-life story, although it sounds very much like a nineteenth-century opera. Charnock leased three villages, Kolikata, Sutanati, and Govindapour, as a trading post for the British East India Company. These three villages later became Calcutta. The couple settled down in the village of Sutanati and are said to have had three daughters. Charnock's tomb, with a Latin epitaph, still stands in the graveyard of St. John's Church, reputedly the oldest building in Calcutta.

Charnock was regarded by the British as the founder of Calcutta, but in 2001 a Calcutta High Court ruling declared that settlements existed on that site long before the arrival of the European settlers. Therefore no particular year can be determined for the city's founding.

The province of Bengal attracted Portuguese, Dutch, French, Danish, and English traders. In 1756 Siraj-ud-daulla, the Nawab of Bengal, confined a large number of Europeans in a small cell overnight without adequate air or water; few survived till next morning—a tragedy that came to be known as the Black Hole of Calcutta. The following year, in the fateful battle of Plassey, the Nawab was defeated by Robert Clive of the East India Company, which marked the beginning of British Raj in India. The Raj lasted two hundred years.

A vibrant city, Calcutta has been home to luminaries such as Rabindranath Tagore, noted film director Satyajit Ray, Swami Vivekananda, famous sitarist Ravi Shankar, and many more. It is also the birthplace of William Makepeace Thackeray, and the site of the world's largest banyan tree. The people of Calcutta are passionately fond of sports, especially football and cricket, and just as fond of food. Calcutta's growth from three small villages to one of the largest metropolises in the world is remarkable. In 2001 the city's name was officially changed from Calcutta to Kolkata, a Bengali version of the name.

Culture Shock in Calcutta

My parents in Calcutta reclaimed me after my grandfather passed away in Bogra, and I was struck with awe at the contrast between the two communities. Calcutta was not a sleepy little town like Bogra, but a large metropolitan city teeming with people, trams, automobiles, radios, and rows of stores on both sides of the street, movie theaters, and noise. I was homesick for Bogra, its slow pace of life, all my wanderings with my friend Phuleswari, and dining with the members of our large joint family. In my mind I could see the gas streetlights of Bogra, and the man with a ladder lighting the lamps in the evening. In Calcutta everything seemed strange, even my two brothers, whom I hardly knew. I felt alienated from my parents and longed to go back to my grandmother and my life in Bogra. I took a long time to adjust to city life.

My two brothers and I used to have snacks after school. Potato croquettes was one of the snacks we loved with tea.

Potato Croquettes with Ground Rice

Serves 4-6
1 lb. potatoes
1 tablespoon butter
1 tablespoon flour
Salt to taste
¼ cup rice
2 fresh green chilies, chopped (optional)
1 cup oil

Boil potatoes, peel them, and mash well with butter, flour, and salt.
Soak rice in water for at least one hour. Drain and make a smooth paste in blender.
Combine potatoes with rice and chopped chilies.

Shape into 2-inch oblong croquettes.

Heat oil and deep-fry the croquettes over medium heat to a golden brown.

Serve hot.

The Fate of a Hindu Widow

Even in the mid-twentieth century the life of a Hindu widow was one of suffering and social exclusion. Sati, the Hindu custom of burning a widow on her husband's funeral pyre as a symbol of her devotion, had been abolished through the tireless efforts of Raja Ram Mohan Roy, culminating in the Sati Regulation Act of 1829. But even after this law was passed, widows, though no longer burnt alive, continued to suffer social humiliation. Their traditional garb was a single piece of rough white cloth with no ornaments. Their hair was cut short, sometimes shaved off, and they led an austere life. Being under strict dietary restrictions, they ate one meal a day, which was lunch. Widows were not allowed to eat supposedly aphrodisiac condiments such as onion and garlic; fish, eggs, and meat were also strictly forbidden. Nor were they allowed to attend any social or religious event like a wedding. This harsh treatment continued until the mid-twentieth century in Bengal.

My Great Aunt, a Widow at Twelve

One of the important family members in my grandfather's household in Bogra was my great aunt, my grandfather's only sister. A child bride, she had been married at the age of eight and widowed at twelve. Her parents brought her back from her husband's family, fearing her in-laws would mistreat her. My family did not share the common Hindu prejudice against widows prevailing at that time. My great aunt held an important position in our large joint family. She observed the dietary rule of a widow, but otherwise led her life like the rest of us. She was consulted on all family matters, and my grandmother was her best friend and confidant. She and my grandmother planned all major celebrations.

She had a large kitchen exclusively for her own use, detached from the main building. It was enormous in size with a large terrace. She used to cook on the terrace, sitting on a flat wooden board with legs 2 inches high. There was also a well for her use only. Through the doors and windows of her kitchen, we children could see rows of large jars of various kinds of chutneys, pithas made from rice wheat flour mixed with sugar, gur or jaggery, and grated coconut, and shelves with other kinds of food that she made for the family consumption. We were not allowed to enter her kitchen, as we ate fish and meat.

According to the custom, my great aunt was a vegetarian and never touched fish, meat, or eggs. An excellent cook, she cooked only vegetarian dishes. Every day at least one item came from her kitchen for family lunch. Sometimes all the children, myself included, would gather in front of her kitchen, and she would distribute pithas or something special to us. We loved her food and called her *Bhalo didi*, which meant good elder sister.

She was a superb storyteller as well. In the evening she told us stories from the *Ramayana* and the *Mahabharata,* I especially liked the story of mighty Bhima from the *Mahabharata* who could uproot a large banyan tree with one hand and chase demons.

My great aunt cooked this potato dish many times. It was full of the aroma of poppy seeds. If you like potatoes, you will love it.

Potato with Poppy Seeds

Serves 4
2 tablespoons poppy seeds
1/3 cup oil (mustard oil preferred)
4 large potatoes, each cut into four pieces lengthwise
1 teaspoon cumin seeds
½ teaspoon turmeric powder
3-4 green chilies
2 bay leaves
Salt to taste

Soak poppy seeds in hot water for two hours. Drain water and make a paste in blender.
Heat oil, and sauté potatoes golden brown. Remove, set aside.
Add cumin seeds to the same oil and stir for a few seconds, and then add poppy seed paste, turmeric powder, green chilies, bay leaves, potatoes, salt.
Lower flame, cover pot, and simmer until potatoes are cooked, about fifteen minutes.

Mixed Vegetables with a Potato Crust

This is really a vegetable pie, cooked with vegetables and *moong dal. Dal* is the Indian word for legumes or lentils. There are at least thirty different kinds of lentils in India, but the most commonly used are *moong, musur, channa,* and *urad.* All are available in Indian groceries. *Moong dal* has a subtle taste and is very easy to digest.

Serves 4

1 cup *moong dal*
Salt to taste
1 teaspoon turmeric powder
4 large potatoes, each cut into four pieces
2 tablespoons butter
1 tablespoon milk
¼ teaspoon pepper
¼ cup oil
1 onion chopped
2 potatoes, diced
1 cup cauliflower, broken into flowerets
1 tablespoon grated ginger
2 cloves garlic, chopped
2 large tomatoes, quartered
½ cup green peas
½ cup sharp cheddar cheese
¼ cup breadcrumbs

Cook *moong dal* (lentils) in three cups of water with salt and ½ teaspoon turmeric powder for 15 minutes on a medium flame. Remove and set aside.
Boil 4 large potatoes, cut into four pieces, mash, and blend with butter, milk, and a little salt and pepper. Set aside.
Sauté onions in oil until light brown.
Add rest of turmeric powder, 2 diced potatoes, and cauliflower, and continue frying with a little sprinkling of water for another 5 to 6 minutes.
Add ginger and garlic, and continue stirring.
Add tomatoes and green peas. Stir for another 2 minutes, then pour lentils into it.

Simmer on a low flame until vegetables and lentils are cooked. (About 10 minutes.)

Grease a baking dish with butter, and pour vegetables and lentils into it. Top it with mashed potatoes, and then sprinkle it with grated cheese and breadcrumbs. Make a smooth layer. Dot it with remaining butter.

Bake in a preheated oven at 350 degrees. for 10 minutes, or until cheese melts.

Okra: The Hibiscus You Can Eat

Okra, belonging to the hibiscus family, is a very common vegetable. It originated in Ethiopia, and then its cultivation spread to the Middle East, India, the eastern Mediterranean, and Africa. Okra is an African word; it is also known as *ochro, bhindi, gumbo, bamia,* and even *ladyfingers,* and a host of other names throughout the world.

Okra arrived in the United States in the eighteenth century with the slave trade, and became essential to Southern cooking, and to the "soul food" of African–American cuisine.

Okra grows in tropical and warm temperate regions. When buying, look for slender, bright green okra, which should break easily at the top. Mature okra gets woody and is not that tasty.

Okra is cooked in many different ways in different regions. In India it is cooked with spices like cumin and coriander. Onion and ginger are often used. Tomato and okra are a perfect match. I prepared this recipe in Calcutta for my two sons, who were teenagers at the time and not particularly fond of okra, but liked this very much.

Stuffed Okra

Serves 4
½ lb. okra
½ teaspoon each of cumin and coriander powder
1 tablespoon finely grated ginger
Salt to taste
½ cup oil

Slit the middle of each okra with a knife, taking care not to cut it in half. There should be a pocket in the center of each okra.

Mix cumin and coriander powder, ginger and salt thoroughly. Using your finger, fill inside of each okra with this spice mixture.
Heat oil, and sauté okra on all sides over a medium flame.

This dish goes well with paratha or rice. Excellent as a snack.

The Land of Six Seasons

A year is divided into four seasons throughout most of the world, but Bengal has six. *Vasanta,* or spring, goes from mid-February to mid-April, *Grishma,* the scorching summer, from mid-April to mid-June; *Barsha,* the rainy season, from mid-June to mid-August; *Sharat,* or autumn, with blue sky, from mid-August to mid-October; *Hemanta,* or late autumn/early winter, from mid-October to mid-December, with bright sun and a nip in the air; and *Seeth or* winter, a dry, cool season, from mid-December to mid-February. In Bengal there are folksongs about the seasons, and festivals to herald each one.

After my marriage I lived in a house in Calcutta surrounded by tall trees called *Gulmohor* or Flame of the Forest. From January to March each tree became a tree of flame, with orange, scarlet, and crimson flowers covering the top. We had a large veranda where I spent a lot of time with my two sons enjoying each season of the year. It was my sanctuary; sitting there, I read, drank tea, and occasionally had meals too with my sons. This veranda was also an ideal place for birdwatchers. Though our house was located in the heart of the city, various species including parrots, quail, cuckoos *(kokil),* woodpeckers, parakeets, myna, and sparrows, just to name a few, were seen perched in the trees. I remember on one beautiful day in early autumn, when I had this vegetable dish while sitting on the veranda watching birds.

Vegetables with Coconut Milk

Serves 4.
2 large potatoes, cubed
1 cup cauliflower, broken into florets
½ cup green peas
1 small white pumpkin (*lau,* available in Indian groceries)
1 cup zucchini, diced
2 tablespoons ghee
1 tablespoon grated ginger
2 cloves garlic, minced
13.5 oz. can coconut milk
4 green chilies
¼ teaspoon each of cinnamon, cardamom, and cloves powder
Salt to taste

Steam potatoes, cauliflower, peas, pumpkin, and zucchini in water to make tender, but not soft. Drain and set aside.

Heat ghee in a pan over a medium flame, and add ginger and garlic. Stir for 30 seconds, add half-cooked vegetables and continue to stir for one minute.

Pour coconut milk over vegetables; add chilies and cinnamon, cardamom, and cloves powder. Blend well.

Add salt.

Cover, and simmer for ten minutes until vegetables are soft.

Spinach Is Two Thousand Years Old

Spinach is said to have originated in Persia (now Iran), where it was cultivated 2000 years ago. It was called *Ispann,* a Persian word meaning "Green Hand." European settlers brought spinach to North America, and it has been popular here ever since.

In India spinach, called *Saag,* is cooked in numerous ways. Versatile, it blends with almost anything—meat, chicken, lentils, and other vegetables—and is excellent as a salad.

Spinach with Almonds

Serves 3-4
¼ cup almonds
2 tablespoons oil
1 teaspoon cumin seeds
1 package chopped spinach
1 tablespoon grated ginger
1 teaspoon turmeric powder
2 tablespoon tomato ketchup
½ cup shredded coconut (available in Indian groceries)
Salt to taste

Lightly sauté almonds in oil, remove, and set aside.
Add cumin seeds to the same oil, stir for 30 seconds, and then add spinach, ginger, and turmeric powder. Continue to stir briskly for two minutes.
Add tomato ketchup, almonds, shredded coconut, and salt.
Stir well, lower flame, cover, and simmer for another ten minutes.

Almonds and spinach make a crunchy dish.

Food Stalls Do a Brisk Business on Sidewalks

There are food stalls along the sidewalks in most of the cities in India. They are located in market-places, movie houses, business districts, railway stations, as well as on any street corner. These food stalls or kiosks are cheap outlets for hot spicy food, especially snacks and tea. These freshly cooked foods are displayed attractively, and passers-by are drawn to them. One of the main items is *pakoras,* which people eat with a cup of tea. *Pakoras* are vegetables deep-fried in batter, an all-time favorite snack. There is always a throng of people around these makeshift kiosks, eating and engaging in friendly conversation. Some cities are concerned about the hygienic condition of these street foods, but the high heat required to cook them presumably kills bacteria.

Spinach Pakora

Serves 4-5

½ cup *besan* (Bengal gram flour)
1 teaspoon baking powder
Salt and pepper to taste
½ cup cold water
1 small package of chopped spinach
½ cup oil

In a bowl mix *besan,* baking powder, salt, and pepper.
Slowly add ½ cup cold water, while stirring all the time to make a smooth paste, avoiding any lumps.
It will be the consistency of a thick pancake batter.
Squeeze out any excess water from spinach, then add spinach to batter.

Heat oil in a pan and drop spinach batter into it with a serving spoon. Saute' both sides of spinach *pakoras* until they turn golden brown. Serve immediately with tomato ketchup. A tasty snack.

Cabbage with Potatoes and Green Peas

This is a very popular dish, simple but exquisite, cooked in almost every home. Whenever I cook it, I remember my mother and grandmother preparing it.

Serves 4-5

1 small green cabbage
2 potatoes, cut into small cubes
¼ cup green peas
1 teaspoon cumin seeds
1 tablespoon grated ginger
2 bay leaves
¼ cup oil
Salt to taste

Cut cabbage into fine shreds.
Heat oil and add potatoes. Sauté over a medium flame until potatoes turn red.
Sprinkle cumin seeds over potatoes, and stir. Add ginger and stir for 30 seconds.
Add shredded cabbage and continue stirring for five minutes.
Reduce flame, add bay leaves and salt.
Cover and simmer until potatoes are cooked.
Add green peas and stir for one minute. Remove and serve with bread or rice.

Fish

Fish (poem)

Ripple
Glide
Bright
Smoothly
Swimming
Splashing
Swiftly gliding, riding over waves
Glistening like a diamond,
Sweeping across oceans,
Sparkling like a bright light,
Flashing in the sunlight,
Glowing like a star,
Stippled and striped.
Swimming as fast as the wind,
Speeding across clear water,
Blue, turquoise, gold, flashing across the seabed,
Jumping merrily escaping man,
Careful! Don't get caught!

Glisten,
Glow,
Glide.

By Annabel Sen, age ten

Bengalis Love to Eat Fish

Bengalis love fish. They eat fish every day at least for one meal throughout the year. Rivers, lakes, and ponds in Bengal are home to several hundred of species of fish. The famous *Hilsa* fish from the river Ganges has a very special place in any Bengali home. *Hilsa* is a seasonal fish, and very bony. One has to master the art of eating it, but its taste is exquisite.

Fish stalls in any food market are situated in a separate section, where only fish are sold. Fish are arranged on tables and the fishmongers weigh, scale, cut, and clean their fish according to the customer's need. There are many types of fish, ranging from the tiniest, about an inch long, to large ones weighing several pounds. Street vendors selling fish roam from one place to another, and ring a bell or shout to announce their presence in the neighborhood.

There are countless recipes for cooking fish in India, especially in Bengal. Bengalis cook fish in mustard oil, which brings out the authentic flavor of any fish.

Dol Jatra: A Festival of Color

Dol Jatra is a Hindu festival dating back thousands of years. It is a colorful festival when cold winter months give way to spring. It is also the time for harvesting, and farmers offer their first crop to Agni, the fire god. In Bengal it is called Dol Jatra or Dol Purnima (Purnima=full moon). It is celebrated in the Bengali month of Phalgun (mid-February to mid-March) on the day of the full moon. Observed all over India, it is known as Holi in the rest of the country.

There are many legends associated with this festival, which signifies the victory of good over evil, and is also connected with the fabled love story of Lord Krishna and his beloved Radha. Lord Krishna celebrated Holi with gaiety and frolic with his band of cowherds and village maidens.

The night before Dol Jatra people collect dry leaves and twigs and burn them in bonfires at crossroads, and sit around the bonfires and sing, accompanied by local musical instruments.

The dry colors originally used to celebrate Dol Jatra were red and green, red symbolizing passion and desire, and green indicating youth and vigor. Now the dry powders come in many shades such as red, pink, green, and yellow. People throw dry colored powder, and carry buckets of colored water and syringes to squirt water in a spray and drench each other.

Dol Jatra is a time of festivity and happiness. Food takes an important part in this community celebration, when people indulge in food, fun, and frolic.

My Great-Grandfather and the Dancing Girls

I heard from my father that his grandfather, who was a landowner and a lawyer in Dacca, now the capital of Bangladesh, lived an opulent life. He heralded spring by throwing lavish parties at his home. Tons of colored powder were dumped on the floor of the Jhalsa Ghar, a room for entertainment where no women of the family were allowed. "Nautch girls" or dancing girls were hired to dance over the colored powder, while all the men were seated on the ground around the raised platform, reclining on huge pillows and smoking hookahs as they watched. Nautch girls were considered immoral and not socially acceptable, but they were in demand even so. Months before the event there used to be passionate discussions among the men about finding the best nautch girls. My great-grandfather always hired them from Lucknow, a city famous for north Indian classical music and dance. As the girls danced, powder flew all over the room, covering the viewers with color. The entertainment was followed by a lunch in full splendor. Family legend says that menus were elaborate, including several fish dishes along with rice, vegetables, meat, and sweets.

A few recipes from this annual spring event of my great-grandfather have been handed down.

Fish Kabab

Serves 6
1 medium onion, chopped
1 tablespoon fresh ginger, sliced
2 cloves garlic, minced
½ cup plain yogurt
6 thick fish fillets
1 teaspoon each of cinnamon, cardamom, and cloves powder
2 fresh green chilies, chopped

1 teaspoon red food coloring
Salt to taste
2 tablespoons ghee or butter
Juice of one lemon

Put onion, ginger, and garlic in blender with a little water and blend into a purée.
Beat yogurt with a fork, then add it to onion purée. Then add fish, and all the cinnamon, cardamom, and cloves powder, and red food coloring, and salt to the purée.
Marinate for an hour. Sprinkle with ghee or butter and put over the grill for 15 minutes. (It can also be cooked over a charcoal fire for barbecues.)
Sprinkle lemon juice over fish before serving.

Bathing in the River Sitting inside a Palanquin

Baishak is the first month in the Bengali calendar. Pahela Baishak is the first day of the Bengali year, which falls on April 14 or 15. The Bengali year is an amalgam of the Indian solar calendar and the lunar year, or Hijri, the Islamic calendar based on lunar cycles, starting on the day when the prophet Mohammed emigrated from Mecca to Medina. The Mughal emperor Akbar introduced this calendar in 1585 to make it coincide with the beginning of the harvesting season, as it was easier for the farmers to pay taxes after crops had been harvested.

An auspicious day among the Bengalis, Pahela Baishak is ushered in with songs, feasts, and other festivities like *mela* (fair). Many people wear new clothes and sing the songs of the great Bengali poet and Nobel Laureate Rabindranath Tagore, such as "Eso Baishak eso eso" (Come, Baishak, come, come), to herald the new year. In keeping with a tradition dating from Akbar's time, business establishments close old books of account, and a special kind of ledger in red cloth binding called *halkhata* is opened, with the offering of sweets to the customers.

On this auspicious day it was customary to bathe in the river to wash one's sins away. My grandmother in Bogra used to do so before starting to cook a festive meal for the family. Since in those days a woman could not be seen in public in wet clothes, she was carried in a palanquin that was dipped in the river and raised again with her sitting inside. After this had been done several times, she returned home to organize a feast.

Many items were cooked. Shrimp with pumpkin, or *lau chringri* as it is called in Bengal, was one of the dishes relished by all.

Shrimp with Pumpkin

Serves 3-4
1 onion, chopped

1 ½ inches fresh ginger, finely sliced
1/3 cup oil
1 teaspoon turmeric powder
½ teaspoon crushed peppercorns
1 13.5 fl. oz can coconut milk
4 green chilies
2 bay leaves
1lb. shrimp, cleaned and deveined
1 lb. white pumpkin (*lau*, available in Indian groceries), cubed into medium pieces
Salt to taste
½ teaspoon cardamom seeds, crushed

Put chopped onion and sliced ginger in blender with a little water and make a smooth purée.
In a pot heat oil over a medium flame and sauté onion and ginger purée, stirring constantly for one minute or until it gets slightly brown.
Add turmeric powder and crushed peppercorns, and stir briskly for one minute.
Stir in half of the coconut milk, the green chilies, and bay leaves.
Combine shrimp and pumpkin, and salt to taste. Reduce heat, cover, and simmer for ten minutes.

Fish with Ground Rice

This is very tasty dish with an unusual combination of flavors.
Serves 6
¼ cup rice, soaked in water overnight
6 thick fish fillets
Juice of one lemon
1teaspoon turmeric powder
¼ cup oil
2 teaspoons fresh ginger, finely grated
2 cloves garlic, finely minced
1teaspoon cumin powder
Salt to taste
1 teaspoon crushed cardamom seeds

Soak rice in water overnight.
Marinate fish fillets in lemon juice.
Sprinkle turmeric powder over fish and cook both sides lightly in oil. Set aside.

Put soaked rice with about ¼ cup water in food processor and blend into a smooth paste.

In a pan heat oil over a medium flame and sauté ginger and garlic for a few seconds.

Add cumin powder with a little sprinkle of water and stir briskly until oil separates from spices.

Add one cup of hot water, fish fillets, and salt to pan. Cover pot and simmer over a low flame for 15 minutes or until fish is cooked.

Stir in ground rice and crushed cardamom seeds and mix thoroughly, taking care not to break fish pieces. Remove from flame.

Ringing the Bell in My Grandfather's Carriage

In the morning my grandfather, a doctor, used to see patients at their homes. This was in Bogra, a small town that is now in Bangladesh. There were no automobiles there at that time, but my grandfather had a horse-drawn carriage, the only means of transportation. Sometimes I used to accompany him on his rounds, but I had to wait outside. I loved to go around the town, sitting on top with the coachman, watching all the sights, and listening to the *clippity clop* of the horses' hooves. It was fun for me to ring the large metal bell of the carriage. The coachman told me when to ring the bell, which warned cyclists and pedestrians on narrow roads of our approach. Often, on our return, we dined on shrimp *malai* curry; he loved it and so did I. Even today it is one of my favorite dishes. It is a typical Bengali dish; every family has its own way of cooking it.

Shrimp Malai Curry

Serves 4
1 large onion, chopped
1 inch fresh ginger, thinly sliced
2 coves garlic, minced
1 lb. jumbo shrimps
1 teaspoon turmeric powder
1/3 cup oil
2 large potatoes, diced
2-inch cinnamon stick, broken into small pieces
4 cloves
1/2 teaspoon cardamom seeds, crushed
½ cup yogurt

1 13.5 fl. oz. can coconut milk
3-4 bay leaves
3 fresh green chilies
Salt to taste
2 tablespoons ghee

Make a purée with onion, ginger, and garlic in blender.
Clean and devein shrimps. Sprinkle a little turmeric powder evenly on shrimps and sauté in oil. Set aside.
Sauté potatoes, set aside.
Add cinnamon, cloves, and cardamom seeds to the oil.
Stir in the onion, ginger, and garlic purée and continue stirring over a medium flame, taking care not to burn it. Stir briskly until spices separate from oil.
Add rest of the turmeric powder and continue stirring, with a little sprinkling of water. Beat yogurt with a fork, add it to spices, and mix thoroughly.
Add shrimps, then coconut milk, bay leaves, potatoes, green chilies, salt, and ghee.
Cover pot and simmer over low heat until shrimps are cooked (approximately 15 minutes)
Serve with rice.

A Pioneer Filmmaker Who Loved Food

My father's uncle, Hira Lal Sen, was a pioneer filmmaker in Bengal. He set up the Royal Bioscope Company in 1898 to distribute his films. I heard from my father and other family members that Hira Lal Sen was obsessed with details in his films, and was also a connoisseur of food. In one of his movies he shot a scene of a feast and was particular about what was being served. Recipes for some of the dishes at that feast have been passed down in my family from generation to generation. Here, with a little modification, is one of the dishes.

Fish Wrapped in Banana Leaves

Serves 6

½ cup shredded coconut
Juice of one lemon
A few fresh cilantro leaves, chopped
3 tablespoons oil
1 tablespoon grated fresh ginger
1 tablespoon cumin powder
6 fish fillets, each about 3 inches long and 1 inch thick
2 fresh green chilies, slit lengthwise
1 teaspoon crushed cardamom seeds
Salt to taste
Banana leaves, if available, otherwise aluminum foil
6 fish fillets
2 tablespoons ghee

Put shredded coconut in a blender with lemon juice and cilantro leaves, blend well, remove.

Heat 3 tablespoons oil in a pan, stir in ginger, cumin, chilies, and cardamom, and sauté one minute, stirring constantly.

Add coconut mixture and stir for another minute. Add salt, remove.

Cut banana leaves or foil into squares each large enough to wrap a fish fillet.

Place each fish on a banana leaf or foil, then put a tablespoon of spiced coconut mixture on top of the fish, and dot with a little ghee. Fold banana leaf or foil around each fillet into a neat package.

Put wrapped fish fillets in a greased shallow roasting pan. Cook in a preheated oven at 350 degrees for 15 minutes or until done.

Serve fish wrapped in banana leaves or foil.

Shrimp Croquettes

Serves 4-5
2 large potatoes
2 tablespoons milk
Pepper and salt to taste
½ lb. medium-size shrimps
2 eggs
2 tablespoons finely chopped cilantro
2 green chilies, chopped (optional)
2 tablespoons flour
Breadcrumbs
½ cup oil

Boil potatoes, peel and mash with a little milk, add pepper and salt. Mix thoroughly.
Clean and wash shrimps. Put in blender and make a purée. Set aside.
Put mashed potatoes, puréed shrimps, one egg, cilantro, and chopped chilies in a bowl, knead lightly, and shape into oblong croquettes.
Roll each croquette in flour.
Lightly beat the second egg with a fork, dip each croquette into egg, and finally coat with breadcrumbs. Deep-fry in oil until the croquettes are golden brown.

This is a snack to look forward to.

The Grandeur of the Past (and Returning Home Hungry)

On weekends I often used to go with my parents and brothers for a sightseeing tour around Calcutta. The old landmark buildings always caught my attention: *Raj Bhavan* (called Government House during British rule), a magnificent building in the midst of acres of garden adorned with sculptures and a massive ornate iron gate; the Victoria Memorial, a beautiful white marble monument surrounded by exquisite gardens; Fort William, enclosed by a 50-foot-deep moat, which was built in 1757, after Robert Clive defeated Siraj-ud-Daula at the battle of Plassey; and the Marble Palace, built by Raja Rajendra Mullick Bahadur in the mid-nineteenth century. Returning home hungry in the late afternoon, we had tea and snacks, and discussed what we had seen. I enjoyed shrimp balls with tea while thinking of those magnificent buildings. Even today I have a vivid memory of those monuments.

Shrimp Balls

Serves 4

¾ cup flour
¾ cup milk
1 egg
1 medium onion, chopped
2 cloves garlic, chopped
2 fresh green chilies, chopped without seeds
A few sprigs of cilantro leaves, finely chopped
½ teaspoon turmeric powder
1 teaspoon cumin powder
Salt to taste

½ lb. medium shrimp
½ cup oil

Make a batter with flour, milk, and egg. Add chopped onion, garlic, green chilies, cilantro, and turmeric and cumin powder, and salt.
Wash and clean shrimp, chop finely. Add shrimp to the batter and mix thoroughly.
In a pan heat oil and pour shrimp batter from a tablespoon, so that each forms a ball the size of a walnut, and place them one inch apart.
Deep-fry shrimp balls over medium heat until they are golden brown.

Fish with Raisin and Pilaf Stuffing

This is a combination of two dishes, fish and pilaf. I have served this dish many times, and each time it won the hearts of my guests. It is also a delight to the eye.
Serves 6/7

1 fish about 5 to 6 lbs. in weight, kept whole
Salt and pepper to taste
Juice of one lemon
2 tablespoons butter
2 tablespoons ghee
1-inch cinnamon stick
3 cloves
4 cardamoms
1 cup Basmati rice
1/3 cup raisins

Have the side of fish cut open by the fishmonger, making a pocket to hold the stuffing. Clean the fish well. Rub it with salt and pepper, sprinkle lemon juice all over the fish and place on a large buttered shallow roasting pan.
Sauté raisins in 2 tablespoons ghee, remove, and set aside.
In the same ghee add cinnamons, cloves, and cardamoms, and then add rinsed rice. Stir briskly for two minutes.
Add boiling water one inch above the rice level. Reduce flame, cover, simmer until rice is cooked and water completely absorbed. Add raisins to rice.
Stuff raisin pilaf inside the fish cavity, sew it with a needle. Melt a little butter and rub it well over the fish on both sides.
Place fish in a preheated oven at 350 degrees for 30 minutes.
Serve on a bed of julienne chips.

Stacey Kaelin

Visiting the Toymaker

My untouchable friend Phuleswari and I often wandered around the town of Bogra, going as far as the riverbank. Sometimes we followed the cry of a bird flying overhead. We crossed many roads, some of them carpeted with fallen leaves, and some mere dirt tracks through the meadows. We watched water buffaloes grazing with birds perched on their back. On our return, very often we stopped at the toymaker's cottage. The toymaker and his wife made toys out of clay, using molds representing various objects like birds, animals, gods, and goddesses. When these were taken out of the molds, they were laid down in the open to dry in the sun. Once the toys were dry, the couple painted them in vibrant colors. I once had several of them, and how I wish I still did!

Returning home, we were ravenous for lunch. I liked rice, lentil, and fried fish, especially with gram flour (lentil flour), which is available in Indian groceries. This dish is very easy and quick to cook.

Fish with Gram Flour

Serves 6
6 fish fillets
Juice of one lemon
1 teaspoon finely grated ginger
½ teaspoon garlic, minced
¼ cup gram flour (lentil flour)
¼ teaspoon ground pepper
½ teaspoon baking soda
A few sprigs of cilantro, chopped
Salt to taste
½ cup oil

Rub fish with lemon juice. Set aside.

Combine grated ginger, minced garlic, gram flour, salt, pepper, and baking powder with a little water to make a thick batter.

Add chopped cilantro to the batter.

Coat fish thoroughly with the batter. Marinate for an hour.

Deep-fry both sides in oil.

Fish Kofta Curry

Serves 4

1 lb. fish fillet
2 bay leaves
2 slices bread
1 teaspoon ground cumin powder
1 tablespoon grated ginger
A few sprigs of cilantro, finely chopped
Salt to taste
½ cup oil
1 large onion, chopped
1 teaspoon paprika
½ teaspoon each of cinnamon, cloves, and cardamom powder
¼ cup plain yogurt

Cook fish with 1 cup water and bay leaves for ten minutes. Drain and mash with a fork.
Soak bread in water and squeeze the water out.
Combine with fish. Add ½ teaspoon cumin, ½ tablespoon grated ginger, half the chopped cilantro leaves, and salt to taste. Form into small balls.
Deep-fry fish balls in oil until golden brown. Remove and set aside.
Sauté onions in the same oil, then add rest of the cumin powder, paprika, and cinnamon, cloves, and cardamom powder, and ginger, and stir over a medium flame until well blended.
Whisk yogurt with a fork and stir into the spices. Stir for a minute; add one cup hot water and salt to taste.
Combine fish balls to the gravy one at a time. Simmer for two minutes. Remove. Garnish with the rest of the chopped cilantro leaves.

India Gained Her Freedom at Midnight

India's independence came at midnight on August 14-15, 1947. I was very young then but felt the excitement all around me. People were buying flags, and my older brother bought an enormous one to fly on our rooftop. At the stroke of midnight, fireworks blazed, ships anchored on the Hooghly River sounded their horns, and patriotic songs blared from radios. Pundit Jawaharlal Nehru, the first prime minister of independent India, gave a speech declaring independence as he hoisted the Indian flag at the Red Fort in Delhi. I still remember his speech broadcast on the radio: "At the stroke of midnight hour, when the whole world sleeps, India will awake to life and freedom."

Next morning it was a day to remember. A big feast was prepared and my mother cooked shrimp cutlets, which we simply loved. This recipe takes me back to my young days in Calcutta when my mother used to make it for us. While she cooked it, the aroma of this delicious dish filled the entire kitchen.

Shrimp Cutlets

Serves 3
6 large jumbo shrimps
1 medium onion, chopped
1 ½ inches fresh ginger, sliced thinly
Salt to taste
2 eggs
Breadcrumbs
½ cup oil

Clean and devein shrimps. Split shrimps, taking care not to disjoint them. Flatten them lightly with the blunt side of a meat chopper, until they look like shrimp butterflies with wings spread.
Put chopped onion and ginger in food processor or blender and make a smooth purée.

Marinate the shrimps in onion and ginger purée and salt for at least two hours in refrigerator.
Lightly beat the eggs and dip each butterfly-shaped shrimp into the eggs and coat them lightly with breadcrumbs.
Over a medium flame sauté shrimp in oil until golden brown.

Spicy Shrimp

Anyone who likes shrimp will love this dish. It has a flavorful taste of spices and goes well with rice, bread, or salad.
Serves 4-6

1 lb. shrimp
1 tablespoon grated ginger
¼ teaspoon each of cinnamon, cardamom, and clove powder
½ cup plain yogurt
1/3 cup oil
Salt to taste

Clean and dry shrimp on an absorbent paper towel.
Combine ginger and cinnamon, cardamom, and clove powder with yogurt and blend thoroughly.
In a pan heat oil and pour in spice mixture, and stir constantly with a little sprinkling of water, until spices separate from oil.
Add salt and shrimp, stir well. Cover pot and cook over low heat for fifteen minutes.
Serve hot with wedges of lemon.

Meat & Poultry

Buying Meat and Poultry

Although India is associated with vegetarianism, two people out of three are non-vegetarian, eating fish, meat, and poultry. The tropical south tends to be more vegetarian, while the consumption of meat and poultry is higher in the north.

In food markets in India, meats are sold in designated separate areas. There are rows of stall, and each stall has one table on which the butchers display different cuts, while carcasses hang from overhead hooks. The butcher stands beside his stall, and tries to get customers to buy from him, and not from his competitors in the neighboring stalls. The customers choose their meat, and the butcher cuts and cleans it, talking about the weather or about the good quality of his cuts, while the customer sits on a stool offered by the butcher. If the customer wants ground meat, the butcher will grind it with his heavy chopper in a matter of minutes. The customer will know that the ground meat does not contain any wastage, that it is made out of lean meat that he or she has selected. The butcher also keeps ground meat prepared beforehand for those who are not so particular.

At the time of festivals, the stalls are decorated with paper streamers and tiny colored electric bulbs. For religious reasons beef, pork, sheep, and goat are not sold in the same stall, but each in a specially designated area. Beef is sold by the Muslims, pork by non-Muslims, and lamb and goat by both Hindus and Muslims. The cattle, sheep, and goats to be slaughtered are all marked with red coloring on their forehead, and are taken out in a long procession to the slaughterhouse, often causing traffic problems on the roads.

Chicken is a popular food in India. Live chickens are available in markets, kept in cages. When a particular bird is selected, it is killed, plucked, and cleaned in front of the buyer. Chickens are also available frozen; the demand for both live and frozen is great.

In food markets eggs stalls are stacked with baskets of eggs. Duck eggs are popular and are used for egg curries. The egg sellers sit in a row on a raised platform with an improvised table lamp without a shade by their side. When a buyer comes, the egg seller holds each egg in front of the lamp, so he can see through it and check its freshness.

In many cities vendors sell live chickens from door to door, and kill and clean them on the customer's doorstep. Peddlers are also seen going from one neighborhood to another with big baskets balanced on their head. Fish and vegetables are also peddled in this way.

When I went shopping in the New Market in Calcutta, I used to go to the same butcher and fishmonger year after year. I developed a trust and knew they would give me only the best meat or fish they had. Their competitors gave up inviting me to their stalls, as they knew I would not buy from anyone else.

Kabab: A Universal Food (and How Swords Turned into Skewers)

Kababs have an instant appeal to the people of any nation. Made mainly of meat, they are tastefully spicy. They came to India at the time of the Mughals. The first of the Mughal rulers in India was Babur, a descendant of Tamerlane and Genghis Khan, who conquered Afghanistan and northern and central India in the mid-sixteenth century. His grandson Akbar the Great expanded the Mughal empire from Afghanistan in the west to Bengal in the east. Akbar's grandson Shah Jahan built the magnificent Taj Mahal, to immortalize his dead wife, Mumtaz Mahal.

Babur loved to eat. He brought melons, peaches, apricots, pistachios, and walnuts from Afghanistan and Persia to India. The superb Mughlai cuisine was created by combining local Indian ingredients with exotic dry fruits and nuts from Persia and Afghanistan, thus bringing gastronomic culture to India. This cuisine features spices and herbs with a garnishing of pistachios, cashews, and raisins. It was the Mughal army that invented shish kabab. Mughal soldiers mounted on horseback used their swords to cut meat into small bite-size pieces, pierced the meat with their swords and, still mounted, held it over fire to cook. This is the origin of modern shish kabab, which is cooked on skewers.

Kababs are of many kinds; some are made of ground meat, and some with meat chunks. Versatile, they can be made of fish or even vegetables, are served at picnics and elegant cocktail parties, and at formal dinner parties and barbecues. In India there are kabab restaurants in every city, and wayside stands on highways selling kabab rolls (kabab rolled in paratha). Kabab shops near movie theaters do brisk business during intermissions, but kababs are served in fashionable restaurants as well. They make a meal by themselves. Parathas are a good accompaniment, or even a simple lettuce salad.

Shish Kabab

When cooking shish kababs on skewers, it is better to thread vegetables or fruits later, as they cook quicker than meat. There are, of course, a few exceptions like small button onions, cherry tomatoes, and green peppers, which can be threaded and cooked at the same time with small lamb or chicken pieces or cubes. Wooden bamboo skewers or sticks should be soaked in water for at least thirty minutes before using. These skewers are inexpensive and easily available. I personally prefer metal skewers, which are reusable and last for years.

Serves 4
1 lb. boneless lamb or beef, cut into 1-inch pieces
1 medium-size onion, ground
1 inch fresh ginger, grated
2 cloves garlic, finely minced
1 teaspoon each of cinnamon, cloves, and cardamom, ground
2 tablespoons plain yogurt
2 tablespoons sour cream
1 teaspoon coriander powder
1 teaspoon poppy seeds powder
¼ teaspoon chili powder
¼ cup oil
Salt to taste
Cherry tomatoes, 2 for each piece of meat
Button onions, 2 for each piece of meat

Marinate lamb or beef with all the above ingredients except the tomatoes and onions for at least two hours or more.
Thread meat pieces on kabab skewers, alternating them with cherry tomatoes and button onions: one piece of meat, then two cherry tomatoes, then another piece of meat, followed by two button onions. Place skewers in a shallow pan. Broil in a preheated oven at 400 degrees until done, basting occasionally with the marinade mixture from the pan. It takes about 20 minutes.
Serve kabab skewers over a bed of plain pilaf.

Plain Pilaf

Serves 4
2 tablespoons ghee or oil
1-inch cinnamon stick, broken into small pieces
3 cardamoms, crushed
4 cloves
1 cup Basmati rice
2 bay leaves

Heat ghee or oil in a heavy pot, add cinnamon, cardamoms, and cloves.
Add rice and sauté it with the spices for a few minutes.
Add boiling hot water 3 fingers above rice level, add bay leaves, cover tightly, and simmer on a low heat until water evaporates and rice is done. Stir with a fork to make it fluffy.

Shammi Kabab: An All-Occasion Food

Soft, crisp, and spicy, shammi kababs are made of ground meat and lentils with spices, and melt in the mouth. A delicacy, they are great for outdoor meals like picnics and barbecues, and for any occasion anywhere.

Shammi Kabab

Serves 4
1 lb. ground lamb or beef
½ cup yellow lentils (chana dal), presoaked
1 tablespoon fresh ginger, finely grated
2 cloves garlic, minced
2-inch cinnamon stick
4 cloves
4 cardamoms
2 bay leaves
½ teaspoon turmeric powder
Juice of one lemon
3 eggs
Breadcrumbs
Salt to taste
¼ cup flour
½ cup oil

In a heavy pan combine all above ingredients except lemon juice, eggs, breadcrumbs, and oil.
Add just enough water to cover ground meat, lentils, and the other ingredients, and cook over a slow heat until meat and lentils are done, about 30 minutes. Remove from flame and discard bay leaves.
Put mixture in blender or food processor without any water and blend into a smooth consistency.
Put mixture in a bowl, add lemon juice and one egg, and knead mixture well.
Add salt and shape mixture into eight patties, each like a hamburger about 2 inches in diameter.
Coat the patties lightly with flour.
Beat the other two eggs, dip each kabab into them, and coat kababs with breadcrumbs. In a skillet put a little oil and sauté kababs golden brown.

Mulligatawny, the Earliest Indian Soup

In traditional Indian cuisine there is no soup. Maybe the Indian custom of eating with the hand prevented a course like soup. Then, in more recent times, Indian restaurants started offering chilled mango-saffron soup, lentil soup, vegetable and other kinds of soup with Indian flavorings, as many people like a soup as a starter.

Though some lentil dishes are liquid in form, they are not eaten as a soup. They are accompaniments to rice or breads. South Indian *rasam* and *sambar,* liquid lentil preparations, can be considered soups, but are eaten with plain boiled rice.

Mulligatawny soup is said to have originated in British households in India during colonial times. The sahibs' craving for soup led their Indian cooks to create a soup with meat and lentils, together with spices and coconut milk, and thus mulligatawny came into existence. The word "mulligatawny" comes from the Tamil (South Indian) word *mulagur tunni,* meaning pepper water. There are many variations. The best I ever had was at the Madras Gymkhana Club in the city of Madras, now called Chennai; the taste still lingers in my memory. Some people consider this a winter soup.

Curry leaves or curry *pata* are essential for mulligatawny soup, as they give a very tantalizing flavor. Curry leaves are available in Indian groceries.

Mulligatawny Soup

Serves 4
1 teaspoon cumin seeds
1 teaspoon coriander
2 large onions, chopped
1 tablespoon grated ginger
2 cloves garlic, minced
2-inch cinnamon stick, broken
6 cardamoms, crushed
4 cloves
2 tablespoons butter
½ lb. boneless lamb pieces
1 cup red lentil (musur dal)
2 bay leaves
A few sprigs of curry leaves
Salt and pepper to taste
1 13.5 fl. oz. can coconut milk
Juice of one lemon

Toast cumin and coriander in a dry skillet, stirring and shaking skillet constantly for 30 seconds. Put in grinder and make a smooth powder.
In a heavy pan sauté onions, ginger, and garlic, then add cinnamon, cardamoms, and cloves in butter. Add lamb pieces and cook until they turn red, about ten minutes.
Add 4 cups boiling water, lentil, bay leaves, curry leaves, salt, and pepper.
Cover pan and bring to a boil, then lower heat and simmer over a low flame until meat is tender. Let it cool. Discard curry and bay leaves.
Put lamb and lentil mixture in blender or food processor and blend to a smooth consistency.
Pour soup in a pot and cook over medium heat for a few minutes, then stir in coconut milk and cumin and coriander powder. Simmer for another 5 minutes.
Serve with lemon juice. A little cooked rice can be sprinkled over the soup.

It is a thick soup, delicious and very filling.

Liver with Coconut

Lamb liver cooked with coconut and spices makes this dish rich and tasty. It goes well with rice or any kind of Indian breads. Coconut cubes are available in Indian groceries; they come in small packages. My mother used to cook this dish quite often in Calcutta, and I simply loved it.

Serves 4

1 onion, chopped
1 tablespoon grated ginger
2 cloves garlic, minced
¼ cup oil
1lb. lamb liver cut into 1-inch cubes
2-inch cinnamon stick, broken into small pieces
4 cloves
1/3 teaspoon cardamom seeds, crushed
1 teaspoon coriander powder
1/3 teaspoon chili powder
20 1-inch cubes of coconut
½ cup yogurt
1 teaspoon turmeric powder
4 green chilies
1 tablespoon tomato ketchup
Salt to taste

Put onion, ginger, and garlic in blender and make a purée. Set aside.
In a pan heat oil and sauté liver cubes for five minutes. Remove and set aside.
In the same oil add onion, ginger, and garlic purée, and stir briskly for a few minutes. Add cinnamon, cloves, cardamom, turmeric, chili powder, and coriander and blend well, stirring constantly.
Add liver and coconut pieces and continue to stir, with a little sprinkle of water.
Beat yogurt with a fork, add to liver and coconut. Blend thoroughly.
Add tomato ketchup, green chilies, and salt to taste. Lower flame and simmer for 10 minutes or until liver is cooked. There should not be too much gravy

How the Parsees Sweetened the Milk

The Zoroastrians, known as Parsees, came to India during the 7th and 8th centuries from Persia (now Iran) to escape religious persecution by the Muslims. They came by ship to the western coast of India and settled in Gujarat. They integrated into Indian society, yet at the same time retained their own culture, customs, and tradition. According to a Parsee legend, when they first arrived on the western coast, the Raja of Sanja sent them a cup of milk full to the rim, which indicated that his kingdom was full and could not take any more people. The Parsees sweetened the milk and sent it back to the king, symbolizing that they would add value to the king and kingdom, and the king then granted them asylum.

Since then the Parsees have indeed sweetened the milk of Indian society. Famous Parsees include J.R.D. Tata, founder of India's first air service, which later became Air India; Sir Ness Wadia, who set up the first wireless service between India and Great Britain; H.J. Bhaba, who launched India's nuclear program; and of course, the world-renowned conductor Zubin Mehta. The Tatas are also the architects of the iron and steel industry in India.

I had a few Parsee friends in Calcutta whom I remember even today for the warmth of their friendship. They wore saris just like us, but occasionally wore Western dresses, too. They were fair-skinned, with good features and friendly disposition. One of my Parsee friends, Frenny, was a marvelous cook; she taught me a lot about Parsee cuisine. We spent many afternoons together, cooking, talking, and laughing.

Dhansak is a classic Parsee dish and very popular, especially in the northwest region of India. There are variations of it, but the basis is a combination of lentils, vegetables, and lamb that gives this dish an unparalleled taste.

Dhansak

Serves 4-5.
½ cup red lentil (moosur)
½ cup yellow lentil (channa dal)
1 small eggplant, diced
½ lb. red pumpkin, sliced into small pieces
½ lb red, firm tomatoes, quartered
1 large onion, quartered
1 teaspoon turmeric powder
½ teaspoon peppercorn
3 bay leaves
Salt to taste
2 lbs. lamb, cut into chunks
½ cup oil
1 large onion, chopped
1 tablespoon grated ginger
2 cloves garlic, minced
2 teaspoons coriander powder
2 teaspoons cumin powder
½ teaspoon cardamom seeds, crushed
¼ teaspoon cinnamon powder
¼ teaspoon cloves powder
½ teaspoon cardamom seeds, crushed

In a pot cook red and yellow lentils, eggplant, pumpkin, tomatoes, and onion with turmeric powder, peppercorn, bay leaves, and salt, with eight cups of water.
Cook until lentils are tender (about 20 minutes). Remove from flame and discard bay leaves.
Put mixture in blender and blend thoroughly. Set aside.
Boil lamb pieces until almost or ¾ done. Remove lamb pieces from stock. Reserve about 1 cup stock.
In a pan heat ½ cup oil, sauté chopped onion to golden brown.
Add ginger, garlic, and coriander, cumin, cinnamon, and cloves powder. Stir-fry for a minute, add ½ cup stock, and cook, stirring all the time.
Add lamb and rest of stock and stir for another minute or until oil separates from meat.
Add lentil and vegetable mixture and crushed cardamom seeds to lamb. Cover pot and cook over a low flame until lamb is tender.

Stacey Krelin

My Great-Grand Father Was Paraded about on an Elephant

My great-grand father was one of the first graduates from Dacca College in the mid-nineteenth century. On the evening of his graduation his family organized a procession for him with much fanfare. He was seated on an elephant, and with drummers beating drums and trumpeters sounding trumpets, the procession went through the entire city of Dacca, and people came out to look at this spectacular sight. After the procession a large number of people were invited to a dinner at his house. Several courses were served, and each course was brought into the dining room with the blowing of a bugle. According to family legend, this was one of the dishes served on that evening. Its succulent delicacy is characteristic of rich Mughlai cooking, which uses spices, nuts, and dried fruit lavishly.

Mughlai Chops

Serves 3
½ cup cashew nuts
1 cup plain yogurt
1 tablespoon grated ginger
2 cloves garlic, minced
1 tablespoon poppy seeds, powdered
½ teaspoon chili powder
½ teaspoon each of cinnamon, cloves, and cardamom seeds, powdered.
Juice of one lemon
½ teaspoon saffron, dissolved in one tablespoon milk
6 lamb rib chops
Salt to taste
1/3 cup oil

1 large onion, cut into thin rings
A large bunch of parsley

Soak cashew nuts in 2 tablespoons water for one hour, put in blender and make a smooth paste.
Combine yogurt with ginger, garlic, poppy seeds, chili, and cinnamon, cloves, and cardamom powder, and cashew paste.
Add lemon juice and saffron. Add lamb chops. Add salt to taste. Marinate for two hours.
Heat oil, cook chops 10 minutes over medium heat. Remove.
Arrange chops in a shallow baking dish, pour gravy from pan over them, and cook in a preheated oven at 450 degrees until meat is tender, about 20 minutes.
Serve with onion rings and sprigs of parsley.

Chicken Pudding

I ate this delicious dish at a small dinner party in Calcutta hosted by my friend Frenny. The dish was smashing and everybody started talking about it. It is a very special dish for grand occasions.

Serves 6

¾ cup oil
4 large onions, chopped
3 cloves garlic, minced
1-inch piece fresh ginger, grated
1 teaspoon cumin seeds, powdered
2 lbs. boneless chicken breasts, cooked and shredded into small strips
4 green chilies
½ cup almonds, sautéed
½ cup raisins
1 quart milk
2 teaspoons sugar
1 cup heavy cream
4 large eggs
Salt to taste

In a pan heat oil and sauté one chopped onion until golden brown.
Add garlic, ginger, and cumin, and cook for a few minutes, stirring.

Add shredded chicken strips, chilies, and salt, and cook for a minute, then add ½ cup boiling water. Remove from fire when a little gravy remains.

Sauté almonds and raisins. Sauté rest of onions separately until crisp and brown. Set aside.

Boil milk until reduced by half. Add chicken and sugar and cook till milk is absorbed in chicken.

In an oiled ovenproof casserole, arrange a layer of chicken, next a layer of onions, almonds, and raisins, and then a layer of cream. Repeat three times, ending with cream. Then spread beaten eggs on top and bake till eggs are set.

Goan Food: A Blend of Many Cultures

Situated on the west coast of India, the city of Goa is famous for its long white sand beaches, which attract tourists from all over the world. Modern Goa is a conglomerate of many civilizations that came in touch with it and influenced its culture. The long period of Portuguese rule in Goa (1510—1961) left a lasting influence on its people and customs, and had a strong impact on their food, which, before the arrival of the Portuguese, was a blend of Muslim and Hindu cooking. This unique mix of different cultures has given a very distinctive taste to Goan food, which is considered the cream of western coastal cuisine.

One of the well-known dishes of Goa is *Vindaloo,* which was brought to Goa by the Portuguese invaders and soon became popular among the people; later it was modified by local ingredients. Historically it was a pork dish cooked with plenty of wine, vinegar, and garlic. Now *Vindaloo* is made of chicken, lamb, and even fish.

For convenience, I have separated the recipe into three parts.

Lamb Vindaloo

Serves 5-6
Part 1. Spices
1 teaspoon coriander seeds
1 teaspoon cumin seeds
1 teaspoon mustard seeds
1 teaspoon fenugreek seeds

Toast spices in a dry skillet, then put them in coffee grinder and make a smooth powder.

Part II. Lamb marinade
5 tablespoons white vinegar

Salt to taste
1 teaspoon brown sugar
4 tablespoons tomato ketchup
2 teaspoons turmeric powder
1 teaspoon chili powder
1 teaspoon paprika
½ teaspoon cardamom seeds, crushed
2 lbs. lamb cubes

Blend coriander, cumin, mustard, and fenugreek powder with white vinegar, salt, brown sugar, and tomato ketchup.
Add turmeric, chili, paprika, and cardamom. Marinate lamb in the mixture for a couple of hours.

Part III. Gravy
2 large onions, thinly chopped
1-inch cube ginger, chopped
4 cloves garlic, finely minced
½ cup oil
4 bay leaves

Put chopped onions, ginger, and garlic in blender with a little water and make a puree. Heat oil and sauté puree, stirring constantly, for about 2 minutes, until puree turns slightly red.
Add lamb with spices to puree and keep on stirring until oil separates from lamb.
Add bay leaves and two cups boiling water, and bring mixture to roaring boil.
Reduce heat, cover tightly, and simmer over a low flame until meat is tender, about 45 minutes to an hour.

Tear-Inducing Onions Are Good for Us

Peaja is an Indian word for onion. *Lamb-do-peaja,* the next recipe, calls for plenty of onions. There are many versions of this recipe in different regions in India. I like to cook it as described here, and it always comes out well. Since a lot of slicing of onions is required for this recipe, be prepared for tears. Why do we cry when we slice or chop an onion? Onions have cells containing sulfuric acid, which in the form of gas irritates the eyes. When onions are sliced or chopped, these cells are broken and release this gas. If onions are chopped when immersed in water, or if you breathe through your mouth, eye irritation can be minimized.

Onions are good for our health. They contain many beneficial plant chemicals, so include an onion in your daily menu. And if you are worried about onion on your breath, remember that eating parsley helps to get rid of the smell.

Lamb-do-Peaja

Serves 4
3 large onions
½ cup oil
1 lb lamb, cut into medium pieces
2 cloves garlic, minced
1 inch fresh ginger, grated
1 tablespoon coriander powder
1 teaspoon black cumin seeds (kalo jeera)
1 teaspoon turmeric powder
½ teaspoon chili powder
½ cup cream
Salt to taste
¼ teaspoon each of cinnamon, cardamom, and clove powder

½ teaspoon coarsely crushed black peppercorns

Slice one onion finely. Heat ¾ of the oil and sauté the onion, then add lamb pieces until lamb is nicely browned.

Add garlic, ginger, and coriander and continue stirring for a few minutes more.

Add black cumin seeds, turmeric, and chili powder. Mix thoroughly, stir in cream and one cup hot water.

Reduce heat, add salt to taste, cover the pot, and simmer until lamb is tender.

Cut each of the remaining onions into four quarters. By hand, separate onion quarters layer by layer.

Sauté onions in the remaining oil for a minute. Do not brown.

Combine sautéed onions with lamb, and stir in cinnamon, cardamom, and clove powder and crushed black peppercorns.

Simmer two minutes. Remove and serve with rice or bread.

Parsee Food, an import from Persia

Frenny, my Parsee friend in Calcutta, was an excellent cook. She loved cooking, and her recipes were either authentic Parsee food or a mixture of Parsee and traditional Indian cooking. The Parsees who settled in India came from Persia, now Iran, and blended their cuisine with Indian influence. Their food makes lavish use of spices like cumin and coriander, and of herbs, especially mint, but it is not chili hot. Meat and eggs have a prominent place in Parsee cooking.

Frenny, a very enterprising woman, started a catering business that catered to most of many elite parties at private homes in Calcutta in winter. She successfully integrated many types of food with her own traditional cuisine to give a different taste and flavor.

This recipe with chicken and macaroni is delicious and yet very simple. These rice macaronis are very small, almost like grains of rice, perhaps a little bigger.

Chicken Macaroni

Serves 4
8 pieces of chicken thighs
1 tablespoon ginger paste
1 teaspoon garlic paste
2 tablespoons coriander seed powder
1/3 cup oil
Salt to taste
1 can tomato purée (half a cup)
1 13.5 fl. oz. can coconut milk
1 package rice macaroni (3/4 of a cup)
¼ teaspoon each of cinnamon, cloves, and cardamom powder

Marinate chicken in ginger, garlic, and coriander for an hour.

In a heavy-bottom pan sauté chicken marinade in oil until brown.
Reduce flame and add 3 cups hot water to chicken, then add salt, and simmer 15 minutes.
Add tomato purée, coconut milk, and rice macaroni, and simmer until chicken is tender.
Add cinnamon, cloves, and cardamom powder before removing from heat.

Football, Blaring Radios, and Lamb

The East Bengal Club and the Mohan Bagan Club have been the two premier football (i.e., soccer) clubs in Calcutta for more than eight decades. Supporters of the East Bengal Club are from East Bengal, now Bangladesh, while Mohan Bagan fans are from West Bengal. The Bengalis are a sports-loving people, so whenever there is a match between these teams, the atmosphere becomes electric with excitement. When I lived in Calcutta the matches were held at the Eden Garden Stadium, which was always filled to capacity. Those who did not get tickets would climb the trees surrounding the stadium to watch the match. Before any major game, heated arguments were heard about who would be the winner. There was a custom in Calcutta that, if the East Bengal Club won, all its supporters would eat *hilsa* fish that evening as a sign of victory; needless to say, that evening the price of *hilsa* fish soared. Similarly, if the Mohan Bagan won, they would celebrate by eating shrimp.

My father was a lifelong fan of the East Bengal Club, as he came from Dacca in East Bengal. He was a very active member of the club and served on its committee for several years. My two sons, who spent a great deal of time with my parents in Calcutta, became passionate about the East Bengal Club at a very early age. Barely 6 and 8 at that time, they sat with their grandpa and listened to the radio commentary. Radios blared from every house in the neighborhood, with thunderous applause and cheers when one of the teams scored a goal. Life came to a standstill, and everyone listened to the radio.

I remember one big match played in the early seventies, when the East Bengal Club won the trophy. The fans went wild with joy and rushed to the fish market to buy Hilsa. We had Hilsa that evening, and the feast continued the next day with this spicy leg of lamb on the menu.

Spicy Leg of Lamb

Serves 8

2 teaspoons cumin seeds
3 teaspoons coriander seeds
5 lbs. leg of lamb
1 tablespoon grated ginger
4 cloves garlic, minced
¼ cup plain yogurt, whisked
4-5 fresh green chilies
Salt and pepper to taste
½ cup oil
½ stick butter
¼ cup almonds, lightly sautéed
4 tablespoons sultana raisins

Toast cumin and coriander in a dry skillet. Grind in coffee grinder.
Trim excess fat from the lamb, and make deep gashes in it.
Mix ginger, garlic, yogurt, cumin and coriander powder, and chilies. Add salt and pepper. Rub spices into leg thoroughly, coating both sides of leg. Marinate overnight in the refrigerator.
Take marinade out of refrigerator, and let it warm to room temperature.
Heat oil and lightly fry the leg on both sides, ten minutes each side.
Place the leg on a shallow baking dish with all the gravy, and butter, and bake for I hour and 30 minutes at 400 degrees.
Reduce to 250 degrees and bake for another 2 hours, basting every 30 minutes.
Place the leg of lamb on a platter, and pour gravy from the baking dish over it.
Garnish with almonds and sultana raisins.

Pantharas: Spring Rolls with a Difference

Pantharas are crepes filled with spicy ground meat dipped in egg, coated with breadcrumbs, and then deep-fried. They are like large spring rolls, but with a different taste. Ground lamb, beef, chicken, or turkey can be used, depending on your preference. A tossed salad of chopped tomato, onion, cucumber, fresh cilantro, with lemon juice, salt, pepper, and extra virgin olive oil go well with *pantharas*. A good brunch dish.

My friend Nargis was renowned for her lavish parties in Calcutta. She came from an aristocratic family from Hyderabad, and her menus reflected the cuisine of that city. I ate *pantharas* at one of her parties, and liked the dish immensely for its versatility: it can be a snack, or a main course with a salad.

Pantharas

Preparations involve (1) crepes, (2) filling, and (3) combining the two.

Crepes

1 cup flour
1 cup milk
2 eggs
¼ cup oil

Combine flour, 2 eggs, 2 tablespoons oil and milk and blend into a smooth pancake batter.
Oil a skillet lightly and pour into it a little batter from a round spatula or milk jug and make thin crepes over a medium flame. Set crepes aside on a warm plate.

Filling

1 small onion, chopped
1 tablespoon ginger, chopped
2 coves garlic, minced
½ cup oil
½ lb. ground meat
2 tablespoons tomato ketchup
1 teaspoon turmeric powder
1 teaspoon cumin seeds, roasted and powdered
4 cloves, crushed
1-inch cinnamon stick, broken into small pieces
½ teaspoon cardamom seeds, crushed
¼ cup raisins, sautéed
A few sprigs of cilantro, finely chopped
Salt to taste

Make a purée with onion, ginger, and garlic. Set aside.
In a pan pour 2 tablespoons of oil and cook onion, ginger, and garlic purée for a minute. Add ground meat, continue cooking while stirring constantly, adding a sprinkle of water, so that meat and purée do not stick to pan. Cook until meat gets brown.
Add tomato ketchup, turmeric, cumin, cloves, cinnamon, cardamom, salt, and a little water. Blend well, lower flame, cover tightly, and simmer for fifteen minutes.
Remove and add chopped cilantro and raisins, and mix thoroughly.

Combining the crepes and filling

2 eggs
Breadcrumbs
Crepes
Filling

Put two tablespoons of cooked meat in center of each crepe. Fold top and bottom of crepe toward center. Fold both sides and form into a roll. They will look like large spring rolls.
Beat the remaining 2 eggs. Dip each *pantharas* into egg, and lightly coat with breadcrumbs. Shake off any excess breadcrumbs.
Use the remaining oil to deep-fry the *pantharas* over a medium flame. They should be golden brown.

Getting Help from a Younger Generation

My grandson Alexander comes to visit us every year from London with his little sister Annabel and his parents. Alexander began making *parathas* with me at the age of six, and by twelve he had mastered it. Annabel is also equally proficient in making this bread. They always have a fun-filled time making dough with flour and rolling out *parathas*. I, of course, cook the *parathas*.

During one of their visits, I made a chicken dish especially for Alexander that he liked very much. I named the dish "chicken Alexander." Alexander is also a poet. Using a theme suggested by one of his teachers, when he was eight he wrote a poem called "The Magic Box."

The Magic Box (poem)

I will put in the box
The first gulp of a newborn baby
A heart from a melting snowman
A seed from a purple-leafed plant.

I will put in the box
The first light of day
The first cold breeze of winter
The first ever ray of light.

I will put in the box
The last leaf of autumn
The last drop of rain
The last heat of summer.

I will put in the box
The last drop of water from a fountain
The last song of the swallow
The last hoot of the hunting owl.

My box is styled from glass and gold
With dragons on the lid,
And secrets concealed
With a lock of rubies.

I shall dream in my box
I shall live in my box and sleep with my own creations.

Chicken Alexander

Serves 4
8 chicken breasts, thinly sliced
3 tablespoons flour
1 stick butter
1 medium onion, sliced
1 ½ cup mushrooms, halved
½ cup heavy cream
Salt and pepper to taste

Lightly coat chicken breasts with flour.
Sauté in half a stick of butter. Remove from pan and set aside.
Sauté onion and mushrooms in butter for two minutes.
Add cream. Season with salt and pepper.
Arrange sautéed chicken breasts in an ovenproof casserole.
Pour onion, mushrooms, and cream over chicken breasts.
Cover it with aluminum foil. Bake in a preheated oven at 450 degrees for twenty minutes, or until chicken is cooked.

It goes very well with rice.

Lamb with Spinach Topping

Serves 4

This is a meat dish with a crunchy crust, combining lamb, spices, and spinach. It can be made with chicken as well.

1 lb. fresh spinach or frozen spinach
1 large onion, chopped
1 tablespoon grated fresh ginger
2 cloves garlic, minced
2 teaspoons coriander seeds
¼ cup raisins
½ cup oil
1 tablespoon ghee
1 lb. boneless lamb cubes or stewed lamb
2 tablespoons tomato ketchup
1 teaspoon turmeric powder
½ teaspoon chili powder
½ cup plain yogurt
2 bay leaves
Salt to taste
½ teaspoon cardamoms, crushed
1 cup coconut milk
2 eggs
¼ cup breadcrumbs
½ cup grated sharp cheddar cheese
1 tablespoon butter

Put spinach in blender for a few seconds until it turns into a purée. Set aside.
Make a purée with chopped onion, ginger and garlic. Set aside.
Toast coriander seeds in a dry skillet, then cool and grind in a coffee grinder.
Sauté raisins in a little oil.
In a pot heat oil and ghee, and sauté onion, ginger, and garlic purée. Add lamb pieces and continue stirring for a while.
Add tomato ketchup, turmeric, chili, coriander powder, and tomato ketchup. Stir briskly for another ten minutes. Whisk yogurt with a fork, and blend into the lamb mixture

Add about 2 tablespoons hot water, bay leaves, salt to taste, and crushed cardamoms. Add coconut milk.

Lower flame and simmer tightly covered until meat is cooked, about 40 minutes. A very little gravy will be left. Remove from flame.

Beat eggs and add to spinach purée. Add breadcrumbs and grated cheese.

Coat a baking dish with butter. Put lamb in it, sprinkle with sautéed raisins, then top the lamb with a layer of spinach and dot it with butter.

Bake in a preheated oven at 350 degrees until it has a crust.

Stacey Koelin

Hyderabad, a City of Mughal Splendor, Technology, and Pearls

Hyderabad is a city on the Deccan Plateau, where north and south India meet. The four-hundred-year-old city is a blend of Mughal splendor and modern technology, as it is now an emerging biotech hub. Hyderabad was besieged and captured by the Mughal emperor Aurangzeb in the seventeenth century. The conquerors built magnificent mosques and minarets and other buildings adorned with stately stucco decorations that are still silent reminders of Mughal grandeur. Hyderabad is also the center of the pearl trade in India and is known as the city of pearls. It has a rich heritage in arts, crafts, and dance, and its cuisine is heavily influenced by the Mughals. Mouthwatering Shahi cuisine of Hyderabad is famous for its aromatic spices and herbs, and its lavish use of dried fruits like raisins, and nuts like pistachios and almonds. Shahi cuisine is truly the cuisine of kings.

Hyderabad Shahi Korma

Serves 5-6
3 medium onions
1 tablespoon grated fresh ginger
3 cloves garlic, minced
½ tablespoon coriander seeds
1 teaspoon black cumin seeds
2-inch cinnamon stick, broken into small pieces
6 cloves
1 teaspoon cardamom seeds
½ cup oil
2 lbs. lamb, cubed
½ cup ghee

2 tablespoons tomato ketchup
2 teaspoons turmeric powder
Salt to taste
3 bay leaves
¾ cup plain yogurt
½ teaspoon saffron threads soaked in a little milk
¼ cup blanched almonds
3 tablespoons heavy cream

Chop one onion and put it in blender with ginger and garlic. Make a soft purée.
Grind coriander and black cumin seeds in coffee grinder.
Grind cinnamon, cloves, and cardamom in the same way.
In a pan heat oil and cook lamb cubes on all sides to a reddish brown. Remove lamb from oil with a slotted spoon and set aside.
Slice the two remaining onions thinly and sauté in the same oil until crisp. Remove and set aside.
Add ghee to oil, then pour onion, ginger, and garlic puree into the pan and sauté over medium heat for a minute.
Add lamb and keep stirring until onion and lamb blend thoroughly.
Add tomato ketchup, then add coriander, black cumin, cinnamon, cloves, and cardamom, and turmeric powder, with a little hot water and stir for a couple of minutes.
Add salt, 2 cups boiling water, and bay leaves. Cover pot, and simmer over low heat until ¾ done (about 30 minutes.)
Beat yogurt and add to it soaked saffron. Add this to meat and blend well. Cover and cook over the same low heat until tender.
Sauté blanched almonds in a little ghee, add them to meat with heavy cream and sautéed onions.

Curry: the National Food of the United Kingdom

The word "curry" is said to be an Anglicization of the South Indian word *kari,* or sauce. The term "curry," meaning stew, is also found in English usage before the British merchants arrived in India.

There is a general misconception that curries are cooked with curry powder, which Americans think is a spice. Actually, curry powder is not one spice but a blend of several basic spices like turmeric, coriander, cumin, and chili, and lets one do Indian recipes using spices from a single package. But authentic Indian recipes are never cooked with curry powder. In India there is a particular plant whose leaves, called curry leaves, or *curry pata,* are used for seasoning, providing a very distinctive flavor.

Bangladeshi immigrants brought their love of curry to Britain, where numerous restaurants serve curry dishes. Chicken *Tikka Masala,* also known as CTM, is the most popular food in the UK, according to Food Service Intelligence, and has been hailed as "Britain's true national dish." Ironically, frozen packages of it are now being exported from Britain to India!

Lamb Curry

Serves 4
1 large onion, chopped
1 tablespoon grated ginger
2 cloves garlic, minced
1 teaspoon cumin seeds
1½ teaspoons coriander seeds
½ cup oil
1-inch cinnamon stick, broken into pieces
4 cloves

¼ teaspoon cardamom seeds, crushed
1 lb. lamb, cut into medium pieces
1 teaspoon turmeric powder
½ teaspoon chili powder
2 tablespoons tomato ketchup
Salt to taste
2 bay leaves
2 potatoes, each peeled and cut lengthwise
1 13.5 fl. oz can coconut milk

Put onion, ginger, and garlic in a blender and blend into a purée.
Toast cumin and coriander in a dry skillet for 30 seconds or until you get the aroma of the spices, shaking the skillet all the time.
Cool, then put in a grinder and make a smooth powder.
Over a medium flame heat oil in a pot and add the onion, ginger, and garlic purée, then add the cinnamon stick, cloves, and cardamom, and stir well.
Add lamb pieces and continue stirring until oil separates from lamb mixture, about 15 minutes.
Add turmeric powder, chili powder, tomato ketchup, and salt, and stir briskly.
Add 1 cup boiling water and bay leaves, lower heat, cover pot, and let simmer.
When lamb is half cooked (about 25 minutes), add potatoes.
When lamb is almost done, add cumin and coriander powder and coconut milk.
Simmer over a medium heat for another 5 minutes. The whole process will take about an hour.

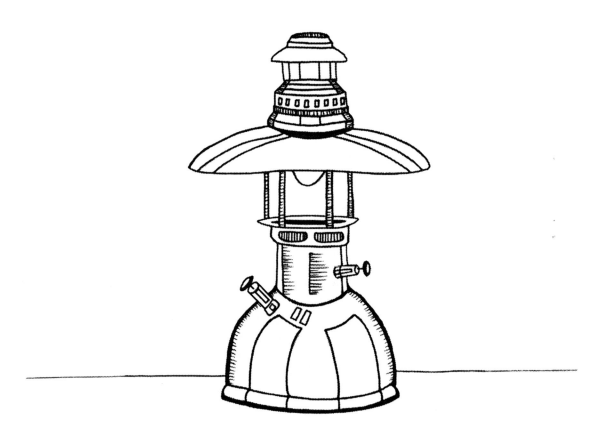

Stacey Kaelin

The Magic of Kerosene Lamps and Gaslight

There was no electricity in the little Bengali town of Bogra when I was living there with my grandparents. In the evening kerosene lamps and petromax lanterns were lit. The lamps were filled with kerosene daily, and the glass of each lamp was cleaned of black soot from the previous night, and wicks were trimmed and adjusted. This was a chore for the servants, who cleaned several lamps every day. Petromax lanterns gave more light than kerosene lamps, but I preferred the lamps, which gave more shadows than light. I used to watch those shadows on the walls; to me they were like imaginary shapes of characters from fairy tales. Gas streetlights also used to fascinate me. Just before sunset a man carrying a ladder climbed to the top of the each lamppost and lit the light. When all the streetlights were lit, they glowed in the darkness, and the streets looked romantic and mysterious, taking me to the *Arabian Nights*.

In our dining room a few petromax lanterns were kept at a certain distance, which gave enough light to dine comfortably. Chicken or lamb was on the Sunday dinner menu, and I loved *chicken rezela*, flavored with yogurt, ginger, and small onions called pearl onions, which we ate in the glowing white light of petromax lanterns.

This is a very tasty dish for those who like ginger and yogurt. It can be made with lamb, and is always slow cooked.

Chicken Rezela

Serves 4.
8 pieces of chicken thighs
2-inches fresh ginger, finely grated
1 cup yogurt
Salt to taste
½ lb pearl onions
4 green chilies

A few peppercorns
1-inch cinnamon stick, broken into small pieces
½ teaspoon cardamom seeds, crushed
4 cloves
½ cup oil
2 tablespoons ghee

In a pot mix chicken with ginger, yogurt, and salt.
Put pearl onions, green chilies, and peppercorns over chicken.
Sprinkle with cinnamon, cardamom, and cloves. Add oil and ghee.
Cover pot and place it on a tray of water in an oven at 350 degrees. Takes about 40 minutes to cook.

It can also be cooked on the stovetop by placing the pot containing chicken in a larger pot with water. It should be simmered.

Desserts

People of India Are Addicted to Sweets

The people of India have an addiction to sweets, which explains the existence of numerous shops in any city or village where sweets are arranged in a very colorful way and look like an artist's palate. It is an age-old custom to offer sweets to indicate success, happiness, or goodwill, or even to welcome a guest. In Bengal, offering sweets to announce good news is a part of the culture.

There are many kinds of sweets and each region offers its own traditional varieties. They come in different shapes, sizes, and colors, but all are delicious. Common Bengali sweets like *rossogolla* and *gulab jaman*, also know as *ledikeni*, are enjoyed by almost everyone in this vast country.

The establishments of some of the legendary Bengali sweet makers are over one hundred years old, with branches all over Calcutta proclaiming the founder's name in boldly lettered signs: BHIM NAG, K.C. DAS, DWARIK GHOSH, GANGURAM. Their secret ingredients are handed down from generation to generation. When Bhim Nag's Sandesh first appeared in the market years ago, it created a sensation. Nabin Chandra Das created *rossogolla*, the ultimate Bengali delicacy, around 1869, and his son K.C. Das made it the national sweet of India. *Lal doi*, or caramel-colored sweet yogurt, is another favorite in Bengal, and all these sweet makers excel in making it.

Rossogolla: A Sweet to Avoid before Exams

Rossogolla originated in Bengal, but is popular throughout India. It is round, white, soft, and spongy, and is soaked in sugar syrup; its taste is unparalleled. When it made its debut around 1869, it immediately won the hearts of all and brought a revolution in the realm of Bengali sweets. However, in our student days we had to refrain from eating it just before an examination, owing to a superstitious belief that if a rossogolla was eaten then, one was likely to get a grade of zero. That is because the shape of this particular sweet is round, and also because *golla* means "round" or "zero." But this sweet is eaten afterward to celebrate success in a test. It is interesting to note, by the way, that the use of zero originated in India.

Rossogolla

Serves 6

1 liter milk
½ teaspoon citric acid or juice of one lemon
2 tablespoons flour
3 cups water
1 cup sugar
A few drops rose water or essence of rose

Bring milk to a boil and let cool. Remove skin of milk.
Boil milk again. Add citric acid or lemon juice, stir until milk curdles completely. This curdled milk is chenna, the main ingredient for rossogolla.
Strain chenna through a fine muslin or cheesecloth. Put a heavy weight on top of muslin to drain out any excess water.
Take chenna out, add flour, and knead into dough. Make small balls.

Boil water and sugar to make a thick syrup. Let cool.

Add chenna balls to syrup, bring to boil again, and cook for ten minutes over low heat.

Remove from stove and cool for a few hours. Add rose water or essence of rose.

How Lady Canning Became Ledikeni

After Rossogolla and Sandesh, the most popular Indian sweet is the irresistible Gulab Jaman, round or shaped like a sausage, deep crimson brown in color, and soaked in syrup. It is everybody's favorite in Bengal and can be found anywhere in India. Gulab Jamun is also known in Bengal as Ledikeni. Lady Canning, the wife of Lord Canning, a governor-general of India in the 1850s, once tasted this sweet and developed a passion for it. Since then it came to be known as Ledikeni, a distorted version of her name, and even today it is called Ledikeni in West Bengal and Bangladesh. Here is a recipe for Gulab Jamun, with a few modifications.

Gulab Jamun or Ledikeni

Serves 6
2 cups sugar
3½ cups water
1 tablespoon rose water
2 cups instant dried milk powder
2 tablespoons self-rising flour
¼ teaspoon baking powder
½ teaspoon cardamom seeds, crushed
½ cup ghee

Make a thick syrup with 3½ cups water and sugar and cook until syrup thickens. Add rose water, cover pot, and set aside.
Mix milk powder, flour, and baking powder with a little water and knead into a soft dough.
Take some dough and make a small ball, about 1 ½ inches in diameter, by rolling it between your palms. Insert a few cardamom seeds in center and roll again into a soft ball. Make six balls in all.

Heat ghee in a pan and cook balls over a low to medium heat to a golden brown. Do not overcook; gently shake pan to let balls get evenly brown on all sides.

Put balls in syrup and let them soak for two hours. Gulab Jamun can be eaten hot or chilled.

Pithas: Homemade Sweets for Festivals

There is a saying that in Bengal there are thirteen festivals in twelve months. Winter festivals are generally celebrated with pithas, which are not available in stores but are made at home. The ingredients include rice flour, flour, grated coconut, milk, sugar, and molasses, or gur, which can be obtained fresh only in winter. There are various types of pithas in different regions of India, representing the culture and tradition of each. In the Bengali winter month of Pous, several kinds of pithas are made to celebrate the harvest; Gokul Pitha, Pathiparsapta, Narus, and Puli Pitha are just a few of them. They are not only tasty, but also a visual pleasure. Because it is time-consuming and laborious, making pithas has become a dying art.

In Bogra, where I was living as a child with my maternal grandparents, making pithas was a big event. All the female members of our large joint family participated in that festive cooking, one of them stirring the milk while another made the filling, and several others grated the coconut. In the month of Pous my grandmother used to make hundreds of them to celebrate the cowherds and the harvest. It was a joyous event, when the cowherds gathered in front of my grandfather's bungalow to take part in the beautiful celebration with a feast of pithas and song.

The Cowherd Festival

In the Bengali month of Pous, which falls in January, a festival was held every year to celebrate the cowherds. In Bogra it was a big event. Early in the morning on a particular day of Pous, all the cowherds gathered in front of my grandfather's bungalow. My grandfather was seated on a chair, and I perched on the arms of his chair, watched and listened as they sang a folksong, while the winter mist dissolved in early sunshine. They sang the same song year after year. I do not remember the words, but I remember the lilting tune.

When the singing was over, my grandfather asked me to give a shiny new coin, a *paisa*, to each of the cowherds. Then my grandmother arrived on the scene, followed by servants carrying large platters of *pithas*, homemade Bengali sweets mainly made of milk and flour. *Pithas* were distributed, and the cowherds sat down on the lush green grass to enjoy them. Weather was always beautiful at that time of the year, crisp, cold, and sunny, with a cloudless blue sky and fragrant flowers blooming all around. I can vividly remember those enchanted moments.

These are some of the *pithas*.

Malpoa

Serves 4-5
1 cup flour
½ cup milk
¼ cup sugar
1 tablespoon fennel
½ cup oil
½ cup sugar
1 cup water
1 tablespoon cardamom seeds, crushed

Blend flour with milk to a thick batter consistency. Add ¼ cup sugar and fennel, mix thoroughly.
Heat oil. Using a round spoon or a milk jug, pour batter into hot oil and prepare small round pancakes.
Sauté pancakes on both sides until crisp and golden brown. Remove and drain on a paper towel.
Combine ¼ cup sugar and 1 cup water to make a thick syrup. Add crushed cardamoms.
Soak pancakes in syrup. Serve either hot or cold.

Gokul Pitha

Serves 4

1 can condensed milk
2 tablespoons flour
½ cup ghee
½ cup sugar
1 cup water
1 teaspoon cardamom seeds, crushed

In a pan cook condensed milk until it gets very thick like a lump.
Make small, flat balls about 1½ inches in diameter. Lightly coat them with flour, and cook in ghee until golden brown.
Make a thick syrup with sugar, water, and cardamom seeds, and put flat balls in it for a few minutes.

Patisapta

Serves 2-3

2 tablespoons ghee
1 cup grated coconut
Jaggery[1]
1 teaspoon cardamom seeds, crushed
½ cup milk
1 cup flour
¼ cup oil

---

1.   For jaggery, or *gur*, see the sidebar on page 153.

In a pan heat ghee and grated coconut and stir-fry.

Add jaggery and crushed cardamom.

Make a batter by combining milk and flour.

Put a little oil in a skillet, then pour in a little batter and spread it all around, like an omelet. Remove batter from skillet and set aside.

Use all the remaining batter to make pancakes. Put coconut mixture in the center of each pancake and roll pancakes lengthwise.

Chandrakath

Serves 3-4
1 can condensed milk
½ cup *suji* (semolina)
1 cup grated coconut
½ cup ghee or oil
½ cup sugar
1 cup water
1 teaspoon cardamom seeds, crushed

Put condensed milk, *suji*, and grated coconut in a pan. Cook mixture until it gets into a thick lump. Let cool, and then make small balls and flatten them, so that each is oblong, 2 ½ inches in length. Sauté in ghee or oil carefully so that they do not break.

Make a thick syrup with sugar, one cup water, and crushed cardamom seeds. Put flat patties in syrup and simmer for 5 to 6 minutes.

There are many kinds of *pithas*; these are just a few of them. *Pithas* play a big role in Bengal, where they are served on special occasions; some are made throughout the year, and some are seasonal. Jaggery, or *gur*, as it is called in India, is used lavishly to make *pithas* in winter.

The Ultimate Delicacy in Desserts

This recipe probably originated in my family. One of my aunts, a culinary expert, introduced it into the family, and my mother took it up with great enthusiasm, making it for special occasions. It is one of the best desserts I have ever eaten, delightfully rich and superb in taste.

Steamed Yogurt

Serves 5-6
2 quarts milk
1 tablespoon lemon juice
1 cup plain yogurt
1 cup sugar
¼ cup raisins
4 tablespoons pistachios, blanched
4 tablespoons almonds, blanched
1 teaspoon cardamom seeds, crushed

In a pan bring 1 quart milk to a boil. Remove and add lemon juice. Let stand for a while to allow milk to curdle.
Drain through a muslin thoroughly. Place a heavy weight over muslin-wrapped curd and press out liquid as much as possible.
Unwrap curd and put in a bowl. Knead curd until smooth. Set aside.
Cook the other quart of milk till reduced by half. Remove from flame.
Add curd, yogurt, and sugar to milk. Blend well.
Stir in raisins, pistachios, almonds, and crushed cardamom seeds.

Coat a round cake tin, pour the creamed mixture in, and cover tightly.
Steam over a tray of water in a preheated oven at 350 degrees until set (about 30 minutes).
Chill thoroughly before serving.

Mango: The Food of the Gods

Mango is the national fruit of India. It is a tropical fruit, and cultivated in India for over four thousand years. The people of India are passionately fond of it. Mango is regarded as the king of fruits, and the sacred book of India, the Vedas, refers to it as "food of the gods."

There are over a hundred varieties of mangoes in India. In the western part of India, Alphasno is the most desired variety, while in Bengal, Langra is everybody's favorite. In summer mangoes flood the markets. Ripe mangoes are eaten, while green mangoes are cooked into chutney and pickles. On hot summer days green raw mangoes with salt help quench thirst. Mango trees are evergreen and grow to a height of 90 feet with a canopy 80 feet wide. The botanical name "Mangifera Indica" confirms their Indian origin.

Alexander and his army were the first Europeans to taste this wondrous fruit during his invasion of India in 327 BC. The famous Chinese pilgrim and traveler Hieun Tsang relished its taste and took the fruit back to China, and the great Mughal emperor Akbar loved it so much that he ordered a thousand mango trees to be planted. It was in the mango groves that Buddha found Enlightenment. Some scholars think that, since apple trees were not native to the region where the story of the Garden of Eden originated, Eve must have tempted Adam with a mango.

Mango leaves and fruit are auspicious in the cultural life of India. Mango leaves are symbols of peace, prosperity, and happiness. Doorways and entrances are decorated with strings of mango leaves to indicate a festive occasion such as a wedding, or the arrival of newborn baby, as well as to invoke good fortune. According to myth, mango blossoms are sacred to the moon and help make wishes come true.

Mangoes have dominated Indian literature, mythology, and arts and crafts. The great poet of ancient India, Kalidasa, paid tribute to mangoes in his writings, and said that the fragrance of a mango blossom is painful to a lovelorn heart. Mangoes are mentioned in the Vedas, the Upanishad, the Ramayana and the Mahabharata. In Indian textiles the shape of a mango has been adapted into the paisley design, which is admired all over the world.

Mango Soufflé

I consider this the king of desserts. It should be light as a feather, and tastes heavenly. Ben Gomez, our cook in Calcutta, prepared the best dishes I ever ate anywhere. A short man with glasses, and soft-spoken, Ben was a skilled professional chef, very focused and quick, deft with his hands, and a marvel to watch in the kitchen.

Serves 4-5
4 eggs
1 cup sweetened condensed milk
Sugar to taste
1 cup heavy cream
1 can mango pulp
1 tablespoon unflavored gelatin

Separate egg yolks and keep egg whites in a glass bowl.
In a saucepan combine condensed milk with egg yolk (lightly beaten) and sugar and make a thick custard over a low flame, stirring constantly. Add heavy cream.
Remove from flame and let cool, then blend in mango pulp.
Dissolve gelatin in 2 tablespoons of water and mix thoroughly into mango mixture with a wooden spoon.
Beat egg whites stiffly until they stand up in a peak. Fold them very slowly into mango custard.
Pour into a round soufflé bowl and chill until set.

Lassi: A Popular Hot-Weather Thirst-Quencher

One hot summer day my American friend Cliff Browder ventured into an Indian restaurant with me and discovered this delicious thirst-quenching beverage. Since then he is an ardent devotee of *lassi*.

It is a popular cooling drink in India, especially in the northern region in summer, when mangoes grow. All restaurants, big or small, serve this drink; even street vendors have a brisk business selling *lassi* to passers-by when the weather is unbearably hot under a blazing sun.

Plain Lassi

Plain *lassi* has the taste of yogurt and lemon, while mango *lassi* has a distinct flavor of yogurt with mango.

Serves 2

1 cup plain yogurt
1½ cups water
1/3 cup sugar
¼ teaspoon salt
Juice of one lemon
A few crushed ice cubes

Put all ingredients in blender and blend at a high speed for one minute.
Serve chilled.

Mango Lassi (or Lussi)

Serves 4
¼ cup sugar
1 cup canned mango pulp
2-3 crushed ice cubes
Juice of one lemon
¼ cup cardamom seeds, crushed
1 cup plain yogurt
A few drops of essence of rose

Dissolve sugar in a little water.
Put dissolved sugar, mango pulps, crushed ice cubes, lemon juice, cardamom seeds, and yogurt in a blender and blend thoroughly.
Pour into glasses and add essence of rose before serving. Serve chilled.

A Winter with Flowers and Fireflies

Winter was never severe in the little town of Bogra. November was pleasant, with a nip in the air and a fragrance of flowers, and meadows were soaked with dew. At dusk folding cots and chairs were set up in front of my grandfather's bungalow. A few log fires were lit to keep us warm, and the surroundings seemed to come alive from a page of an adventure story. The fields around Bogra were infested with snakes, and now, looking back, I think the fires were meant also to keep snakes away. Lying on one of the cots, I would look at the sky sprinkled with stars, and try to count them. My grandmother used to make suji coconut patties, an all-time favorite snack that was often served to the evening campers. We ate this delicious snack by the glow of the fire, while watching the dancing flames, and twinkling fireflies in the distant bushes.

Suji Coconut Patties

Serves 3-4

1 cup ghee
1 cup suji (available in Indian groceries)
1 cup grated coconut
1 cup milk
1 cup sugar
½ cup sautéed raisins
1 teaspoon crushed cardamom seeds
1½ cup flour
Pinch of salt

Heat ¼ cup ghee and sauté suji, then add grated coconut and stir briskly until brown. Add ¼ cup milk, reduce heat, add ½ cup sugar, and continue stirring. Add rest of milk, until suji and coconut turn completely brown.

Stir in sautéed raisins. Remove from fire. Add crushed cardamom seeds. Set aside.

Sift together 1 ½ cups flour, a pinch of salt, and 1 tablespoon ghee. Make dough with cold water; form into balls, and on a floured surface roll out thin rounds, about three inches in diameter.

Place suji coconut mixture in center of each flour round, and fold in half to form into a patty. Pinch edges to seal.

Deep-fry both sides of each patty in rest of the ghee to a golden brown.

Prepare a thick syrup with one cup of water and ½ cup sugar.

Dip patties in syrup and allow at a few hours before serving.

This is both a dessert and a snack.

A Parsee Wedding with Fire

The Parsees are a close-knit community of the Zoroastrian religion, which is more than three thousand years old. Their ancestors migrated to India from their motherland of Persia (now Iran) during the seventh and eighth centuries to avoid religious persecution by the Muslims. Most of them settled in Gujarat, on the western coast of India, and in some neighboring states. Today they are pioneers and leaders in technology, medicine, law, music, and education. Their food is spicy, rich, and tasty, but it is not readily available in restaurants.

A Parsee wedding is performed by priests according to the Zoroastrian tradition, with symbolic items like mirrors and candles, and with songs and prayers. The ceremony begins four days before the wedding. Traditionally the bride and groom are dressed in white and wear flower garlands around their necks. Marriage prayers are said by priests who shower them with rose petals and rice, and the marriage is solemnized in front of a fire. A grand feast follows the ceremony.

I attended a Parsee wedding reception in Calcutta. It was an open-air reception on an evening in late autumn with a number of guests, most of them Parsees. The women wore beautiful saris with jewelry, and some of the older women wore saris in a different way, bringing the end of the sari over the right shoulder instead of the left. The men wore Western clothes. There was a vast array of food, all of it delicious, but the real treat was the traditional wedding custard.

Parsee Wedding Custard

Serves 6

1liter milk
1 can condensed milk
6 eggs, separated
A few drops of vanilla essence
½ teaspoon cardamom seeds, crushed
1 cup sugar
2 tablespoons butter or ghee
½ cup golden raisins

Boil milk until reduced by half. Let cool, add condensed milk.
Beat egg yolks lightly, add to milk.
Add essence of vanilla, crushed cardamoms, and sugar. Mix thoroughly.
Beat egg whites stiffly and fold in the mixture.
Coat a round baking dish with butter or ghee and pour mixture into it. Bake in a preheated oven at 400 degrees.
When mixture is half set, sprinkle almonds on top, then continue baking until custard is set, and top gets light brown (about 30 minutes).
Sauté raisins in a little butter or ghee. Sprinkle raisins on top of custard.

Happy Birthday with Rice Pudding

Rice pudding, or *chaler payesh* (*chal* = rice), is a very common dessert in Bengal, and a must for celebrating a birthday. The person whose birthday is celebrated should eat rice pudding at the end of the main meal on that day.

The ideal rice for *payesh* is *Govindabhog,* a small-grained, fragrant variety. Since it is hard to find outside of India, Basmati is a good substitute.

Rice Pudding *(Chaler Payesh)*

Serves 4-5
½ cup rice
1 quart milk
2/3 cup sugar
2 teaspoons rose water
½ teaspoon cardamom seeds, crushed
½ cup sautéed raisins

Rinse rice; soak it in plain water for an hour. Boil milk for five minutes, slowly add rice to it.
Over medium heat cook rice in milk with sugar, stirring for ten minutes.
Lower flame and cook over a low heat until rice is cooked and milk thickens.
Add rose water and crushed cardamom seeds, stir well.
Remove from flame and put sautéed raisins on top. It should be thick and creamy.

Gur, a Different Kind of Sugar

Gur or jaggery, a dark, unrefined sugar from the juice of a certain date palm, is popular throughout southeast and southern Asia. Gur can be liquid, or solid in round blocks; if solid, it is easily broken. It is widely used in Indian cooking, mainly in preparation of sweets, but also in savory dishes. The taste of gur is different from sugar, having a sweet winy taste. Its flavor lends a distinctive taste to other foods. Gur is the healthiest sugar in the world, containing proteins, minerals, and vitamins, and is used in Ayurvedic medicine. In many parts of India it is considered to be auspicious and is used in ceremonies. Gur is available in Indian groceries and can be stored for a long time.

In winter, when gur appears in the market, people in Bengal look forward to sweets made with natun gur or new jaggery. Broken and mashed into small pieces, gur is added to rice pudding just before the pudding is ready, giving the pudding a nice coffee color and a sweet taste of molasses. When using gur, reduce the amount of sugar and add gur, broken into small pieces, stirring briskly. In Bengal gur is a key ingredient in the preparation of pithas.

How My Grandmother Entertained Unexpected Guests (When Not Fighting Snakes or Catching Thieves)

My grandmother, the matriarch of our large joint family in Bogra, was a wonderful woman. When a family member or a neighbor fell sick, she nursed them day and night. A good storyteller, she kept us children mesmerized with her tales from mythology.

Grandmother was also quite courageous. Walking between the big house and her bungalow in the evening, she beat off any dangerous snake on her way with a cane. And once, when she and my great aunt went looking for a stray sheep at night, they discovered a thief hiding under a bench. When he leaped up and darted off, my great aunt shrieked and fled, but my grandmother chased after him. The thief had greased his naked upper body with oil, so when she grabbed him, he slipped out of her grip and escaped.

An excellent cook, grandmother had full control over our big kitchen. When my grandmother used to make *halwa*, a tantalizing aroma came from the kitchen and flowed all around, making us aware of a great treat to come. This is very simple to cook, and takes less than half an hour to prepare. It needs to be stirred vigorously all the time, so it doesn't get burnt or stick to the pan. Both my mother and grandmother used to make it for unexpected guests. Hospitality in India is legendary, and it is an important aspect of Indian culture to treat both invited and uninvited guests with respect.

Suji Halwa

Serves 3-4

¾ cup *suji*
½ cup ghee or oil
2 cups milk
½ cup raisins, sautéed
1teaspoon cardamom seeds, crushed

In a heavy-bottomed pan fry *suji* with ghee over medium heat, stirring briskly until it turns completely brown.
Slowly add milk.
Add sugar and sautéed raisins.
Remove from heat when it thickens.
Sprinkle on crushed cardamoms and serve hot.

Carrot Cake (Gajjar Halwa)

My next-door neighbor in Calcutta was passionate about this cake and made it so many times that she perfected the art of making carrot cake. She used to put silver paper or *tabak* on top of the cake, giving it a silvery appearance; this paper is available in Indian groceries.

Serves 4-5

2 lbs. carrots, finely grated
1 quart milk
¾ cup sugar
¼ cup butter
1 teaspoon cardamom seeds, crushed
½ cup raisins, lightly sautéed
½ cup almonds, lightly toasted
1 sheet silver paper

In a heavy pan cook carrots with milk and sugar over low heat until milk is completely absorbed in carrots.
Stir butter into carrot mixture and continue stirring for a minute. Add crushed cardamom seeds and stir well. Remove from flame.
Put carrot mixture in a shallow dish and spread raisins and almonds over it. Chill thoroughly.
Put silver paper on top of carrot cake before serving.
Serve with whipped cream or vanilla ice cream.

I Encounter a King Cobra

It happened on one hot summer night in Bogra, a sleepy little town with broad green meadows and trees, when I was six years old. I was living there with my maternal grandparents. Bogra was notorious for snakes, big and small, so one had to be careful when walking around after sunset. Because of the heat, that night my grandmother had made a bed for me on the floor, next to the four-poster bed, where it was cooler. There was no electricity, but in one corner a solitary kerosene lantern dispelled darkness. Fast asleep, I woke up to find myself held tight in my grandmother's arms. She was standing on the four-poster, shouting. Later I heard the story.

When my grandmother walked into the bedroom, to her horror she found a cobra coiled on my pillow, its hood slowly swaying over my head. Keeping her gaze fixed on the snake, she slowly approached, scooped me from the floor, and jumped up on the high four-poster. The snake chased us and, trying to climb up, coiled around one of the legs of the bed. When my grandmother cried for help, two of our relatives came running with guns and shot the snake.

The news of a cobra swaying over my head spread all around, and many people rushed in to see the dead cobra and me. The huge cobra was displayed hanging from a piece of wood, and the air was charged with excitement. Always ready to create myths and legends, the townsfolk thought that the cobra, far from wanting to harm me, was in fact protecting me; clearly, this little girl would grow up to be someone exceptional! (I'm afraid I've disappointed them.) Delighted by their prediction, the next day my grandmother invited them over for a feast of sweets. She later told me several varieties of sweets were made, and coconut *burfi* was one of them.

Coconut Burfi

Makes 15-20 sweets
3 tablespoons ghee
1 package shredded coconut
1 cup sugar

¼ cup condensed milk
½ teaspoon cardamom, crushed
½ cup golden raisins, lightly sautéed

Heat ghee in a pan and add coconut.
Cook coconut, stirring, until it gets brown.
Add sugar and continue stirring briskly for ten to fifteen minutes.
Add condensed milk and stir for another ten minutes until a soft dough is produced.
Add cardamom and raisins. Mix well.
Coat a flat tray or a plate with a little ghee, and press coconut mixture firmly onto it. Set aside for an hour.
Cut into squares and serve.

978-0-595-46158-5
0-595-46158-1

CPSIA information can be obtained at www.ICGtesting.com
Printed in the USA
LVOW111021120213

319733LV00003B/12/A

9 780595 461585